CW01020204

A PRACTICAL INTRODUCTION TO IN-DEPTH INTERVIEWING

SAGE was founded in 1965 by Sara Miller McCune to support the dissemination of usable knowledge by publishing innovative and high-quality research and teaching content. Today, we publish more than 750 journals, including those of more than 300 learned societies, more than 800 new books per year, and a growing range of library products including archives, data, case studies, reports, conference highlights, and video. SAGE remains majority-owned by our founder, and after Sara's lifetime will become owned by a charitable trust that secures our continued independence.

Los Angeles | London | Washington DC | New Delhi | Singapore | Boston

A PRACTICAL INTRODUCTION TO IN-DEPTH INTERVIEWING

ALAN MORRIS

Los Angeles | London | New Delhi
Singapore | Washington DC | Boston

Los Angeles | London | New Delhi
Singapore | Washington DC | Boston

SAGE Publications Ltd
1 Oliver's Yard
55 City Road
London EC1Y 1SP

SAGE Publications Inc.
2455 Teller Road
Thousand Oaks, California 91320

SAGE Publications India Pvt Ltd
B 1/I 1 Mohan Cooperative Industrial Area
Mathura Road
New Delhi 110 044

SAGE Publications Asia-Pacific Pte Ltd
3 Church Street
#10-04 Samsung Hub
Singapore 049483

© Alan Morris 2015

First published 2015

Apart from any fair dealing for the purposes of research or private study, or criticism or review, as permitted under the Copyright, Designs and Patents Act, 1988, this publication may be reproduced, stored or transmitted in any form, or by any means, only with the prior permission in writing of the publishers, or in the case of reprographic reproduction, in accordance with the terms of licences issued by the Copyright Licensing Agency. Enquiries concerning reproduction outside those terms should be sent to the publishers.

Editor: Katie Metzler
Assistant editor: Lily Mehrbod
Production editor: Victoria Nicholas
Copyeditor: Jen Hinchliffe
Proofreader: Kate Campbell
Marketing manager: Sally Ransom
Cover design: Shaun Mercier
Typeset by: C&M Digitals (P) Ltd, Chennai, India
Printed in Great Britain by Henry Ling Limited at The Dorset Press, Dorchester, DT1 1HD

Library of Congress Control Number: 2014953937

British Library Cataloguing in Publication data

A catalogue record for this book is available from the British Library

MIX
Paper from
responsible sources
FSC
www.fsc.org   FSC™ C013985

ISBN 978-1-4462-8729-3
ISBN 978-1-4462-8763-7 (pbk)

At SAGE we take sustainability seriously. Most of our products are printed in the UK using FSC papers and boards. When we print overseas we ensure sustainable papers are used as measured by the Egmont grading system. We undertake an annual audit to monitor our sustainability.

For Sue, Sophia and Jeremy

CONTENTS

About the author   ix
Acknowledgements   xi
Preface   xiii

1   The what and why of in-depth interviewing   1

2   Ethics – the need to tread carefully   17

3   Developing the interview guide   39

4   Selecting, finding and accessing research participants   53

5   Preparing for the interview   69

6   Conducting the interview   79

7   Dealing with difficulties and the unexpected   99

8   Transcribing, analysing and writing up the interviews   121

Index   139

ABOUT THE AUTHOR

Alan Morris is an urban sociologist based in the Australian Centre of Excellence for Local Government, at the University of Technology, Sydney. He has a PhD in Sociology from the University of the Witwatersrand in South Africa. His PhD was a major qualitative study of inner-city transition in Johannesburg during the final years of apartheid. The book, based on his PhD, *Bleakness and Light: Inner-City Transition in Hillbrow, Johannesburg* (1999, reprinted 2001), is viewed as one of the key South African texts in urban studies. In Australia his main research focus has been on the impact of housing tenure on older people who are dependent on the age pension for their income. His research interests include housing, ageing, urban marginality and social policy. He has published extensively in peer-reviewed journals in Australia, the United Kingdom, the United States and South Africa.

ACKNOWLEDGEMENTS

A few people have helped this book along. Sasindu Gamage and Benjamin Hanckel read all the chapters and provided very useful feedback. Benjamin also generously shared a couple of his own personal interviewing experiences, which I have included in the book. The Director of the Australian Centre of Excellence for Local Government at the University of Technology, Sydney (UTS), Roberta Ryan, gave me the time and space to write the book. This is much appreciated. Jillian Rose applied her superb formatting skills to great effect. I received excellent advice on ethics from Racheal Laugery who is based in the Research & Innovation office at UTS. My editor, Katie Metzler, was always constructive and encouraging and was a pleasure to work with. The various reviewers certainly helped improve the final product and their critical comments are appreciated. Finally, I want to thank all the people I have interviewed over the years. It is a privilege entering into people's lives, albeit for a short period of time. I have learnt a great deal and on many occasions have been inspired and moved by their graciousness, insights and resilience.

PREFACE

The book is geared towards aspiring social science researchers who have never done a study based on in-depth interviews or who have done some interviewing but have found the method and analysis daunting. It goes through every facet of conducting a study based on interviews and draws on actual studies to illustrate the challenges and possibilities. My hope is that by the end of the book you should feel confident enough to go out into the field to experience and enjoy this potentially extremely powerful and rewarding method. Reading the book will facilitate your progress but it is only by venturing out and interviewing that you will hone your skills.

In the first chapter I give a brief history of the interview and discuss its strengths and weaknesses as a method. I also discuss the different kinds of interviews. However, the focus in this book is on the in-depth semi-structured interview.

The second chapter discusses ethics. All institutions require that you obtain ethics approval prior to conducting your interviews. The chapter outlines the essentials of conducting ethical research and discusses the ethics application process. The ethics in the writing up of interviews is also examined. Chapter 3 discusses how to go about constructing an interview guide and what questions to ask, what questions not to ask and the order of questions. The interview guide is only a guide, but it is important that you have a clear sense of what themes you want to cover in the interview. A common problem with studies based on interviews is establishing who to interview and then recruiting interviewees. In many studies recruitment can be a major task. Of course, it does depend on the nature of the study. Chapter 4 examines the selection, finding and accessing of interviewees.

Chapter 5 is a practical but important chapter. It talks about the basic requirements for a successful interview. The importance of good equipment, dressing appropriately and finding a suitable venue tend to be underestimated. Many interview studies fail due to the interviews conducted not yielding much data. Although it is inevitable that interviews will vary in quality and some will be disappointing, there are ways to maximise the possibility that the interview will be successful.

Chapter 6 discusses ways to optimise the possibility of your interviews yielding rich data. Interviewing is rarely a smooth process and it is not unusual for the interview to go awry. Chapter 7 suggests ways that you can salvage interviews that are going poorly. It also discusses the challenge of interviewing across difference. Every interview is a co-construction between the interviewer and the interviewee. The sex, race, ethnicity, sexual orientation and class of the interviewer/interviewee can make a difference to the trajectory of the interview. Difference is not necessarily negative. However, what is essential is that there is reflexivity on the issue. The final chapter examines the post-interviewing phase – transcribing and writing up the interviews. The focus is on thematic analysis. A challenge is writing up the interviews in an interesting, rigorous and appealing way. This is a daunting and time-consuming task. However, there are methods you can adopt to facilitate the task and these are discussed.

1

THE WHAT AND WHY OF IN-DEPTH INTERVIEWING

In-depth interviewing is the most common qualitative research method. This is not surprising as when it is done well it is a powerful way to gather data. This chapter gives a brief history and definition of the in-depth interview and reviews its advantages and limitations. The question of when to use in-depth interviews is then discussed. The different kinds of in-depth interviews are summarised. The chapter concludes by reflecting on the current debate around the authority of the data obtained from interviews. Chapter headings include:

- A brief history of the interview in social research
- What is an in-depth interview?
- The strengths of in-depth interviews
- The limitations of in-depth interviews
- When to use in-depth interviews
- The different approaches to interviews
- Increasing reflexivity of the interview in the contemporary period

A BRIEF HISTORY OF THE INTERVIEW IN SOCIAL RESEARCH

Interviewing as a method to understand our social world has a long history. Probably the first use of interviews in social research was Charles Booth's seminal study of poverty in London in the 1880s. Much of his data were obtained from interviews he conducted with School Board Visitors (SBVs) in the poverty-stricken

East End of London. The job of the SBVs was to keep a record of children in the households to which they had been assigned. When a child failed to attend school, they were expected to visit the household and establish the reasons for non-attendance. This would involve interviewing the parents. Acute poverty meant that school attendance was poor and as a result SBVs over a period of time accumulated an intimate knowledge of the households they were responsible for. Booth conducted hours of interviews with the SBVs in order to acquaint himself with their exhaustive knowledge of the circumstances of the households in question (Bales, 1994). Noteworthy is that Booth refused to interview the actual residents. He walked through the areas under study but did not enter any homes, noting that to do so would be 'unwarrantable impertinence' (in Bales, 1994: 345).

In the United States of America, as early as 1924, Emory Bogardus, Professor of Sociology at the University of Southern California, wrote that interviewing is 'one of the important methods now being used in social research ...' and in 1926 he published what is considered to be the first detailed account of in-depth interviewing as a method (Bogardus, 1926). In his seminal 1924 article on interviewing, he lists the various kinds of interviews that were already well established at this time – 'The physician, the lawyer, the priest, the journalist, the detective, the social worker, the psychiatrist and the psychoanalyst make regular use of it' (Bogardus, 1924: 456).

In the realm of psychiatry, Sigmund Freud's (1856–1939) pioneering work on psychoanalysis and the role of the unconscious was based on interviews with his patients over an extended period. Freud used free association – a particular and unusual variant of the interview. Unlike ordinary conversation, free association requires that patients do not censor themselves but instead say whatever comes to mind however unpleasant or embarrassing. This method, Freud argued, allows the analyst to access the unconscious of the patient – 'the pure metal of valuable unconscious thoughts can be extracted from the raw material of the patient's associations' (Freud, 1905: 112).

However, in the social sciences in the first part of the twentieth century there was still a great deal of doubt about using interviews as a method. The interviewing of ordinary citizens was viewed with scepticism. Class prejudice encouraged the perception that ordinary citizens would mislead the interviewer. W.I. Thomas, the joint author of the early classic, *The Polish Peasant in Europe and America*, commented,

> Interviews may be regarded as part of personal observation, but the ordinary inhabitant has a singular interest in misleading the outsider and putting a different face on things. (Thomas, 1912: 771–2 in Lee, 2008: 312)

It was only in the late 1930s that the in-depth interview started gaining recognition as an acceptable method in the social sciences (Lee, 2008). In 1939, Pauline V. Young in her book, *Scientific Social Surveys and Research*, wrote,

> The personal interview is penetrating; it goes to the 'living source.' Through it the student … is able to go behind mere outward behaviour and phenomena. He [*sic*] can secure accounts of events and processes as they are reflected in personal experiences, in social attitudes. He can check inferences and external observations by a vital account of the persons who are being observed. (in Platt, 2001: 36)

In the contemporary period, in-depth interviewing is undoubtedly the most used qualitative method (Denzin, 1989; King and Horrocks, 2012). It is now so ubiquitous as a method and a means to understand our social world that social researchers talk about the 'interview society' (Atkinson and Silverman, 1997; Gubrium and Holstein, 2001; Kvale and Brinkmann, 2009). Besides being at the core of social research, through television, radio, print media and the internet we are constantly exposed to the interview as a mode of obtaining information and opinions.

WHAT IS AN IN-DEPTH INTERVIEW?

The semi-structured in-depth interview (I will be focusing on semi-structured in-depth interviews in this book) is similar to a conversation in that there are two individuals discussing a topic of mutual interest and ideally the discussion is relaxed, open and honest (Mason, 1998). In essence, it involves a researcher asking questions and following up on the responses of the interviewee in an endeavour to extract as much information as possible from a person (the interviewee) who has expertise on the topic/s the interviewer is interested in. This expertise is usually premised on the interviewee having direct experience of the topic under review and produces what Kvale and Brinkmann (2009) have called 'interview knowledge'. The in-depth interview ideally should be a flexible and free-flowing interaction in which the interviewer allows the interviewee a good deal of leeway. However, the interviewer also directs the conversation as discreetly as possible so as to ensure that the interviewee conveys as much relevant information as possible in the time allocated and covers the topics that have been designated by the interviewer as important. Interviewees are able to express themselves in any way they desire. The expectation is that they tell their story in their own words. Unlike a conversation, in a research interview there is far more probing by the interviewer. A probe involves asking interviewees to elaborate or explain an answer. It is an endeavour to obtain more clarity and detail on a particular topic.

The length of interviews varies. Usually an hour appointment is made, but ultimately the time taken depends mainly on the depth of interviewee's answers, the topic and the skill of the interviewer. Some interviewees will give detailed and elaborate answers and the interviewer does not have to do much besides keep the interview on track. Some topics lend themselves to interviewees giving rich answers. For example, once you have gained their trust, there is little doubt that a person who has endured domestic violence will have a good deal to say. An inexperienced interviewer is less likely to adequately probe than a skilled experienced interviewer and is also more likely to interrupt inappropriately. Probing and the degree to which an interviewer should intervene are discussed in detail in Chapter 6.

Some qualitative researchers argue that one interview with an interviewee is not enough and that in-depth interviewing should involve 'repeated face-to-face encounters between the researcher and informants ...' (Taylor and Bogdan, 1984: 7). Multiple interviews are almost always done when the research involves a longitudinal study (Grinyer and Thomas, 2012). There are clear advantages to doing multiple interviews (see Earthy and Cronin, 2008) but the disincentive is that it is time-consuming and costly. Also, in many instances interviewees will not be prepared to give up more time. Many studies are based on one-off interviews with interviewees.

Although, ideally, the in-depth interview should be conducted face-to-face, it can be done by telephone, Skype or email. These modes, discussed in detail in Chapter 6, allow the interviewer to extend the geographical ambit of potential interviewees and can be as effective as face-to-face interviews.

An in-depth interview in the social sciences is a peculiar phenomenon for several reasons. The person being interviewed is expected to 'open up' and divulge information to the interviewer despite the fact that in almost all cases the latter is a stranger and is not necessarily expected to disclose much about themselves. The interview often involves the asking of questions that are personal and which the interviewee may never have discussed with anybody or even thought about. Also, the interviewer is likely never to see the interviewee again. In contrast to everyday conversation, the interviewer is usually in control of the interaction and decides whether the questions have been satisfactorily answered and when the interview should conclude. Another unusual feature is that the interviewee is expected to give up a significant amount of their time. A key feature of the interview in social research is that the information given is confidential and deidentified, whereas in everyday conversation this is rarely the case. Gossip and indiscretion are common components of everyday conversation (Conein, 2011).

THE STRENGTHS OF IN-DEPTH INTERVIEWS

In-depth interviewing, when done competently, is a highly effective method for obtaining data for social research. In contemporary society the way people live their lives, the issues they face, their experiences and how they see and make sense of the world are extremely varied and not necessarily evident to the researcher. Also, differences in terms of status, income, wealth, ethnicity, age, sexual orientation and lifestyle, combined with massive population concentrations, mean that there will be a good deal of social reality which is not part of the researcher's immediate experience. You may have little knowledge of the lives of single parents in public housing, older renters, young rappers, ex-prisoners and women who have experienced domestic violence. On the other side of the continuum you will probably have limited knowledge of the lifestyles or perceptions of wealthy households. The interview gives the researcher access to interviewees' thoughts, reflections, motives, experiences, memories, understandings, interpretations and perceptions of the topic under consideration. It gives the researcher the opportunity to establish why people construct the world in particular ways and think the way they do. The stories of interviewees are 'a way of knowing' (Seidman, 2013: 7).

In my own research, interviews have been an indispensable source of data. I have used them extensively and in the process have had the privilege of accessing the world of the unemployed, corporate and slum landlords, irate tenants, small business owners, age pensioners, anti-apartheid activists, sex workers, homeless people and immigrants who have experienced threatening xenophobia. It is possible to get an idea of how people see the world through the use of a survey questionnaire, observation, blogs and secondary sources, but the strength of the in-depth interview lies in its ability to create a research space in which the interviewee is able to tell their story and give the researcher a range of insights and thoughts about a particular topic. Through in-depth interviews the researcher is able to obtain an understanding of the social reality under consideration and, depending on the circumstances, collect rich data fairly rapidly.

It is an extremely versatile method and can be used to study an almost limitless range of topics and research questions. For example, Cashmore and Parkinson (2011) used in-depth interviews with high conflict separated parents who had been instructed by a Judge to attend a 'Contact Orders Program'. The Program is designed to help parents who have a history of contravening the child-care arrangements that have been put in place by the courts. The main focus of the study was to examine 'the history and nature of the parents' disputes, and their experience of the court system … and their response to the program of therapeutic mediation' (Cashmore and Parkinson, 2011: 187). A key finding was that with high conflict families traditional ways of settling disputes – mediation, court based conciliation and negotiation between lawyers – are unlikely to have any impact. The distrust and animosity is too deep. The 20 interviews elicited powerful perceptions that could not have been obtained in any other way.

A study of the motivations of child soldiers by Brett and Specht (2004) was based on 53 in-depth interviews with child soldiers from ten countries. The key research question was what made children decide to become child soldiers? The authors found that there were common factors that pushed these children to become soldiers, but that each interviewee also had their own unique motivation. The interviews established that all of the child soldiers came from poor households and disrupted families. However, many children who come from similar circumstances do not become soldiers. Thus in order to understand what makes one child join and another child not join, the authors concluded that it was essential that we go beyond environmental factors and understand the child's personal history.

A similar study based on in-depth interviews on why young men in Nigeria joined armed groups found that besides a fear of being attacked and the perception that they needed to defend their communities, a key motivation was the sense of shame if they did not join. Family, peer and community pressure was enormous. 'Soldiers' were also promised that they could keep any spoils of war – a major incentive in this poor area (Barrett, 2011)

The material generated through in-depth interviewing can make an impact on public perceptions. A study I did with a colleague on the impact of living on Australia's paltry unemployment benefit (it is called 'Newstart') generated much interest when it was reported on in the mainstream media. This was mainly due to the poignant quotes of the interviewees as they described the impact of living on the minimal unemployment benefit. There was much financial stress, their housing was often dire, social isolation was common, their physical and psychological health was poor and their capacity to re-enter the workforce was substantially weakened by their lack of resources (Morris and Wilson, 2014). A survey could illustrate that a large proportion of Newstart recipients could not afford a range of items but would not be able to pick up the multifaceted and detailed nature of the impacts. As Rubin and Rubin (2012: 3) argue, interviewing people 'can challenge long-held assumptions and help recast ineffective public policies.' Perhaps our research on Newstart recipients may make a contribution to altering the perception that the unemployment benefit needs to be kept below the poverty line so as to coerce people back into employment.

THE LIMITATIONS OF IN-DEPTH INTERVIEWS

Like any research method, in-depth interviews do have limitations. An important limitation is that the interviewee has the ability to construct a world the veracity of which is usually difficult to check (of course, questionnaire surveys are not immune to this phenomenon). Thus a person may say that they have strong social ties whereas in actual fact they are lonely and feel isolated. The only way this statement can be verified is by participant observation or by interviewing people who have sound knowledge of the interviewee. However, these verification tools are often not possible or practical. The issue of accuracy and the degree to which the interviewee's account reflects the social reality under consideration has to be constantly reflected on. However, in most instances, if the interviewee feels comfortable with the interviewer, they will endeavour to give what they consider is an accurate portrayal (Rubin and Rubin, 2012). There is no doubt that in every study based on in-depth interviews there will be interviewees who will hold back and not give a comprehensive and/or accurate account of events.

Another limitation is that data obtained from interviews cannot be generalised to the population. Although interview data can suggest a definite pattern, you always need to hedge its generalisability.

Interviewing is potentially a time-consuming and expensive method. Accessing interviewees, in some cases, may be difficult and involve much effort. The transcribing of interviews can be arduous if you do it yourself and, if you pay a professional, it can be costly.

The strengths and limitations of in-depth interviews are summarised in Figure 1.1.

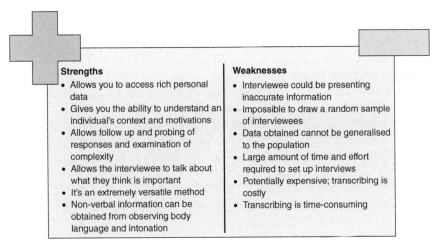

Strengths
- Allows you to access rich personal data
- Gives you the ability to understand an individual's context and motivations
- Allows follow up and probing of responses and examination of complexity
- Allows the interviewee to talk about what they think is important
- It's an extremely versatile method
- Non-verbal information can be obtained from observing body language and intonation

Weaknesses
- Interviewee could be presenting inaccurate information
- Impossible to draw a random sample of interviewees
- Data obtained cannot be generalised to the population
- Large amount of time and effort required to set up interviews
- Potentially expensive; transcribing is costly
- Transcribing is time-consuming

Figure 1.1 *Strengths and weaknesses of in-depth interviews*

WHEN TO USE IN-DEPTH INTERVIEWS

It is difficult to have definitive guidelines as to when in-depth interviews are appropriate. It is such a powerful method that it is probably safe to argue that in almost every social research situation they may have a role to play. Certainly, when the research involves obtaining a sense of how individuals view their situation and what their experiences have been around the research topic under consideration, in-depth interviewing is an appropriate method. The interview allows us to enter the interviewee's 'lived everyday world' (Kvale and Brinkmann, 2009: 29).

In-depth interviewing is usually an appropriate method for sensitive topics. If you are examining the experience of racism and how people cope, the in-depth interview gives you the opportunity to establish a rapport with the interviewee before exploring potentially personal and difficult material (Mellor, 2003). A study on the impact of the holocaust on survivors would require personal face-to-face contact with the interviewer and the interviewee (Greene, 2002). It is unlikely that an impersonal questionnaire survey would capture the trauma and be welcomed by survivors.

The research question you are investigating is a key gauge of whether you should or should not use in-depth interviews. Any research question that can be answered by people talking about their experiences lends itself to in-depth inter-viewing. If you are interested in the question, 'How do interruptions of doctors in emergency departments impact on patients?' then observation and recording of the interactions between the doctors and nurses and others, will probably be a more powerful method and more appropriate than in-depth interviews (see Chisholm et al., 2000). If your research question involves trying to capture what the population thinks about a particular issue, a questionnaire survey is a more appropriate method than in-depth interviews. For example, Wilson and Meagher (2008) were interested in investigating how 'Australians perceived increasing ine-quality in Australia since the mid 1980s in a context of strong economic growth'. Drawing on surveys on social inequality and on social attitudes conducted in 1987, 1992, 1997, 2002 and 2005, they found that while Australians were increasingly concerned about the growing gap between rich and poor, a far smaller proportion thought it was the job of government to do something about the gap and redistribute income (Wilson and Meagher, 2008: 232).

A major advantage of questionnaire surveys is that if the sample is adequate and has been randomly selected, the findings can be generalised to the popula-tion. A questionnaire survey can measure how respondents feel about particular issues but the capacity of surveys to explain why respondents feel the way they do is limited.

In-depth interviewing can be complemented by participant observation, analysis of census data, document analysis, video analysis, surveys, etc. Bergman (2008: 18) concludes, 'using data of different types can help us both to determine what interpretations of phenomena are more or less likely to be valid and to provide complementary information that illuminates different aspects of what we are studying'. Thus a survey questionnaire could be followed by in-depth interviews or vice versa (see Creswell, 2003). The questionnaire survey can generate key demographic data and allow us to obtain some understanding of a situation while the in-depth interviews allow the researcher to probe beyond the surface findings of the survey. In my own research on inner-city transition in Johannesburg, I first did a random survey of residents and followed this up with in-depth interviews. The interviewees were drawn mainly from the respondents to the survey. The survey allowed me to gather a substantial amount of data that could be generalised to the population. The interviews brought the data to life; interviewees were able to tell me about their everyday lives in an area that was the first urban space to experience the collapse of enforced racial segregation in Apartheid South Africa (Morris, 1999).

THE DIFFERENT APPROACHES TO INTERVIEWS

Interviewing can take different forms. They can be precisely structured with set questions, semi-structured or unstructured. Although the different kinds of interviews are presented as 'pure' categories, there is often overlap.

The structured interview

The structured interview is closely aligned to the survey method. Structured interviews have set questions and the interviewer is expected to stick to the questions set and the order of questions. There is no expectation that the interviewer probes the answers given or digresses from the set questions. Rather, the emphasis is on minimising interviewer effects by training interviewers to ask questions in a standardised fashion and to limit their non-verbal responses. The central premise is that interviews must be standardised as much as possible so as to eliminate interviewer variation and error. In the structured interview, questions are generally closed rather than open-ended. In other words interviewees are presented with a range of predetermined possible answers to questions set. If there is scope for follow up questions, these are usually standardised.

A good deal of attention is also paid to potential issues such as the gender and 'race' of the interviewer (Schaeffer et al., 2010). If the structured interviews are being conducted in a poor, black neighbourhood it is desirable that the interviewers be black so as to avoid bias. If the topic is domestic violence and the abuse of women, it is important that the interviewers are female. Interviewers are also not expected to reveal much of themselves so as to avoid 'social desirability bias'. This occurs when interviewees give interviewers the answers they feel the interviewer will want to hear (Esterberg, 2002).

In-depth, semi-structured interviews

In-depth semi-structured interviews are semi-structured in that the interviewer has topics that they want to cover that are related to their research question/s, but there is plenty of scope for digression. The interviewee is allowed to 'ramble' to an extent and the interview style is conversational. However, the interviewer is expected to cover all the key topics in the interview guide (see Chapter 3) and intervene when appropriate. The semi-structured interview also gives the interviewer the space to seek clarity as to what the interviewee actually means and why they gave a particular answer. There is thus scope for a detailed discussion. For example, if an older private renter feels that the agent or landlord is treating them unfairly, the semi-structured interview allows the interviewer to explore and establish the reasons as to why the interviewee has this perception.

In many interview situations there is the space and need to probe. For example, if you are investigating gender dynamics in gangs the semi-structured interview will give you the scope to delve into the different ways men and women experience gang dynamics. Miller and Brunson (2000) interviewed 58 gang members in St Louis (31 men and 27 women); a key finding was that the proportion of girls in a gang played a major role in determining their experience. In gangs where girls were a distinct minority, the young women tended to identify strongly with the male members and male dominance tended to be excessive. In gangs where young women were well represented, the male–female dynamics were not as overtly sexist – '... girls received status and protection in the gang' (Miller and Brunson, 2000: 439).

Semi-structured in-depth interviews can be repeated so as to build up the rapport between the interviewer and interviewee and enhance the depth and detail of the answers.

Unstructured interviews

In unstructured interviews or open interviews there is not necessarily a pre-given list of topics and interviewees are encouraged to answer at length. The questions asked give the interviewee the opportunity to give detailed answers and explanations and to set the agenda for the interview; 'In unstructured interactive interviews, participants retain considerable control over the process' (Corbin and Morse, 2003: 337). The unstructured interview is often accompanied by observation, and questions arise in context. For example, Schultze (2000) spent eight months doing a field study in the headquarters of a US manufacturing firm examining how knowledge workers produce information and what it involves. Besides observation and informal conversation she had regular unstructured interviews with the participants in the work context. The situation triggered the questions. The unstructured interview is similar to a real conversation in that the context is crucial and there is a fair amount of spontaneity.

Narrative interviews

With narrative interviews there is an endeavour to get interviewees to tell their story about a particular event or issue as a narrative or a story. There is a good deal of overlap with life histories, as interviewees will be asked to organise their presentation temporally. There is minimal interruption by the interviewers when the interviewee tells their story and selects what they see as important. Often narrative interviews have a significant historical component, comprising an interviewee reflecting back on their life to explain an event and its consequences.

Holloway and Jefferson (2000: 4) contend that the narrative interview is more powerful than the semi-structured interview as it gives the interviewee the chance to 'free associate' and thereby make connections which they would not have thought about or been prepared to reveal if the researcher was using the standard semi-structured interview method. They argue that when interviewing people about painful experiences a common phenomenon is the 'defended subject'. The defended subject or interviewee is reluctant to share painful experiences with an interviewer when the standard question answer interview mode is used. Rather they will attempt to manage these painful experiences by giving basic and vague answers. One way to address this is to ask questions that are very open-ended and which encourage the interviewee to tell a story related to the topic and talk about whatever is on their mind. Interruptions are kept to a minimum.

Life history interviews

The life history interview gives the interviewee the space to tell their life story and key events are focused on. It gives the interviewer the capacity to assess why the interviewee is in a particular situation – for example, in an abusive relationship, in and out of prison or a religious cult. In the area of public health, the life history interview has been used to examine how the lifestyles of individuals impacts on their health and what would be appropriate interventions (Goldman et al., 2003).

Usually the life history interview will be guided to some extent by the interviewer. It does, therefore, overlap with the semi-structured interview. However, the telling of their life story and what they focus on is left to the interviewee. It is their story.

The life history interview requires a good deal of trust between the interviewer and the interviewee as the latter is expected to give a comprehensive and honest account of their lives and some of the events discussed could induce painful memories.

INCREASING REFLEXIVITY OF THE INTERVIEW IN THE CONTEMPORARY PERIOD

Over the last couple of decades there has been an increasing questioning of the interview as a method. Historically, it was viewed as an unproblematic method that elicited information that represented the interviewee's reality. There was consensus that the responses of interviewees represented the 'real world' and there was little need to interrogate the views, perceptions, experiences and feelings expressed in the interview. This approach has been labelled a realist perspective. A realist perspective is similar to the perspective of social scientists using survey questionnaires. There is a reality out there that you can accurately capture and represent.

The argument that the in-depth interview necessarily accurately captures the interviewee's reality has been subjected to much scrutiny. There is increasing acceptance that cognisance needs to be taken of the interviewer–interviewee relationship and the way it can impact on the interaction and the answers of the interviewee. Invariably the interaction will be influenced by contextual factors such as the age, ethnicity, gender and class of the interviewer and at times, the setting. This is discussed in detail in Chapter 7. What is required is that the interviewer recognises the potential influence of these factors and endeavours to ensure that bias is minimised.

The constructivist perspective emphasises the relative nature of knowledge – 'at different times and places there will be different and often contradictory interpretations of the same phenomena' (King and Horrocks, 2012: 22). In relation to interviews, the constructivists argue that the interviewee constructs a particular view of reality and that this view is shaped fundamentally by the interview itself. Thus, 'Respondents are not so much repositories of knowledge – treasuries of information awaiting excavation – as they are constructors of knowledge in collaboration with interviewers' (Gubrium and Holstein, 2003: 68). The answers an interviewee gives to one interviewer will probably be different to the answers they give to another interviewer. What the constructivist approach does is heighten our sensitivity to the centrality of the interviewer–interviewee relationship and the interview process. The responses of interviewees will be shaped by the interviewer's questions, the relationship of the interviewer with the interviewee and the context. The interview is thus viewed as a collaborative process – the content, to an extent, is shaped by the interaction. The extent to which the interviewee trusts the interviewer, the questions asked, the level and kind of probing and the interruptions will all contribute to shaping the final product – the interview transcript. During the course of the interview, the interviewee consciously and unconsciously makes decisions to omit some experiences, perceptions and insights and not others, to give varying degrees of detail and perhaps exaggerate some aspects and downplay others. In sum, the interviewer can only try their professional best to elicit material that reflects the interviewee's reality. You can never be totally sure that you have succeeded.

SUMMARY

This chapter introduces the reader to in-depth interviewing. The brief history of the interview in social research illustrates how the interview as a method has historically been viewed with much scepticism and it was only in the late 1930s that the interview emerged as a recognised method in the social sciences. In contemporary social science, the in-depth interview is the key qualitative method. In essence, the in-depth interview is a conversation that is directed by the interviewer. Although the interviewee has leeway to digress, ultimately the aim of the interview is to shed light on the research questions the interviewer is endeavouring to answer. The advantages of the interview are highlighted. It is argued that if your research question requires accessing an individual's personal experience, understandings and perceptions, then an in-depth interview is potentially a highly effective method. However, in-depth interviews do have limitations. A key limitation is that the interviewee can give limited or even misleading answers. Also, the data obtained cannot be generalised to the population. These limitations can be dissipated by combining in-depth interviewing with other methods. Although the in-depth semi-structured interview is the focus of this book, the different forms interviewing can take are briefly reviewed. Finally, the chapter discusses the increasing reflexivity around the interview as a method and the varying ways interview material is viewed. The interviewer needs to be aware of the factors possibly influencing the interviews – reflexivity is essential.

Exercise

List five studies where in-depth interviews would be an appropriate method to use. Explain your reasons for choosing these studies.

REFERENCES

Atkinson, P. and Silverman, D. (1997) 'Kundera's immortality: the interview society and the invention of the self', *Qualitative Inquiry*, 3 (3): 304–25.

Bales, K. (1994) 'Early innovations in social research: the poverty survey of Charles Booth', PhD dissertation, London School of Economics, London.

Barratt, R.S. (2011) 'Interviews with killers: six types of combatants and their motivations for joining deadly groups', *Studies in Conflict & Terrorism*, 34 (10): 749–64.

Bergman, M.M. (2008) 'The straw men of the quantitative-qualitative divide and their influence on mixed methods research', in M.M. Bergman (ed.), *Advances in Mixed Methods Research*. London: SAGE. pp. 11–21.

Bogardus, E.S. (1924) 'Methods of interviewing', *Journal of Applied Sociology*, 9, 456–67.

Bogardus, E.S. (1926) *The New Social Research*. Los Angeles: J.R. Miller.

Brett, R. and Specht, I. (2004) *Young Soldiers. Why they Choose to Fight*. Boulder, Colorado: Lynne Rienner Publishers.

Cashmore, J.A. and Parkinson, P.N. (2011) 'Reasons for disputes in high conflict families', *Journal of Family Studies*, 17 (3): 186–203.

Chisholm, C.D., Collison, E.K., Nelson, D.R. and Cordell, W.H. (2000) 'Emergency department workplace interruptions: are emergency physicians "interrupt-driven" and "multitasking"?', *Academic Emergency Medicine*, 7 (11): 1239–43.

Conein, B. (2011) 'Gossip, language and group size: language as a bonding mechanism', *Irish Journal of Sociology*, 19 (1): 116–31.

Corbin, J. and Morse, J.M. (2003) 'The unstructured interactive interview: issues of reciprocity and risks when dealing with sensitive topics', *Qualitative Inquiry*, 9 (3): 335–54.

Creswell, J.W. (2003) *Research Design: Qualitative, Quantitative and Mixed Methods Approaches*. London: SAGE.

Denzin, N. (1989) *The Research Act.* Englewood Cliffs, NJ: Prentice Hall.

Earthy, S. and Cronin, A. (2008) 'Narrative analysis', in N. Gilbert (ed.), *Researching Social Life.* London: SAGE. pp. 420–39.

Esterberg, K. (2002) *Qualitative Methods in Social Research.* Boston: McGraw-Hill.

Freud, S. (1905) *Fragments of an Analysis of a Case of Hysteria.* London: The Hogarth Press.

Goldman, R., Hunt, M.K., Allen, J.D., Hauser, S., Emmons, K., Maeda, M. and Sorensen, G. (2003) 'The life history interview method: applications to intervention development', *Health Education and Behaviour*, 30 (5): 564–81.

Greene, R.R. (2002) 'Holocaust survivors: a study in resilience', *Journal of Gerontological Social Work*, 37 (1): 3–18.

Grinyer, A. and Thomas, C. (2012) 'The value of interviewing on multiple occasions or longitudinally', in J.F. Gubrium and J.A. Holstein (eds), *The SAGE Handbook of Interview Research: The Complexity of the Craft.* Thousand Oaks, CA: SAGE. pp. 219–30.

Gubrium, J.F. and Holstein, J.A. (2001) 'From the individual interview to the interview society', in J.F. Gubrium and J.A. Holstein (eds), *Handbook of Interview Research: Context and Method.* London: SAGE. pp. 3–32.

Gubrium, J.F. and Holstein, J.A. (2003) 'Active interviewing', in J.F. Gubrium and J.A. Holstein (eds), *Postmodern Interviewing.* Thousand Oaks, CA: SAGE. pp. 67–80.

Holloway, W. and Jefferson, T. (2000) *Doing Qualitative Research Differently: Free Association, Narrative and the Interview Method.* London: SAGE.

King, N. and Horrocks, C. (2012) *Interviews in Qualitative Research.* London: SAGE.

Kvale, S. and Brinkmann, S. (2009) *Learning the Craft of Qualitative Research Interviewing.* London: SAGE.

Lee, R.M. (2008) 'Emory Bogardus and the new social research', *Current Sociology*, 56 (2): 307–20.

Mason, J. (1998) *Qualitative Researching.* London: SAGE.

Mellor, D. (2003) 'Contemporary racism in Australia: the experience of Aborigines', *Personality and Social Psychology Bulletin*, 29 (4): 474–86.

Miller, J. and Brunson, R.K. (2000) 'Gender dynamics in youth gangs: A comparison of males' and females' accounts', *Justice Quarterly*, 17 (3): 419–48.

Morris, A. (1999) *Bleakness & Light: Inner-City Transition In Hillbrow, Johannesburg.* Johannesburg: Witwatersrand University Press.

Morris, A. and Wilson, S. (2014) 'Struggling on the Newstart unemployment benefit in Australia: the experience of a neoliberal form of employment assistance', *Economic Labour Relations Review*, 25 (2): 202–21.

Platt, J. (2001) 'The history of the interview', in J.F. Gubrium and J.A. Holstein (eds), *Handbook of Interview Research: Context and Method*. Thousand Oaks, CA: SAGE. pp. 33–54.

Rubin, H.J. and Rubin, I.S. (2012) *Qualitative Interviewing: The Art of Hearing Data*. London: SAGE.

Schaeffer, N.C., Dykema, J. and Maynard, D.W. (2010) 'Interviewers and interviewing', in P.V. Marsden and J.D. Wright (eds), *Handbook of Survey Research*. Bingley: Emerald Group Publishing Limited. pp. 437–70.

Schultze, U. (2000) 'A confessional account of an ethnography about knowledge work', *MIS Quarterly*, 24 (1): 3–41.

Seidman, I. (2013) *Interviewing as Qualitative Research: A Guide for Researchers in Education and the Social Sciences*. New York: Teachers College Press.

Taylor, S.J. and Bogdan, R. (1984) *Introduction to Qualitative Research Methods*. New York: Wiley.

Wilson, S. and Meagher, G. (2008) 'Richer, but more unequal: perceptions of inequality in Australia 1987–2005', *Journal of Australian Political Economy*, 61: 220–43.

2

ETHICS – THE NEED TO TREAD CAREFULLY

Ethics has become a central part of social research. In this chapter I briefly discuss the context in which ethics has emerged as a primary concern. The principles and procedures for conducting research in an ethical fashion are then discussed. Some time is then spent on the practicalities of obtaining ethics approval from your institution. The issue of ethics does not end with institutional approval. The ethical issues that can arise during the course of the interview and in the writing up phase are examined. Chapter headings include:

- Why ethics?
- The key principles and procedures for conducting research ethically
- Applying for ethics approval from your institution's Ethics committee and the decision-making process
- Responding to an initial request from the Ethics committee for clarification
- How to prevent and respond to ethical issues arising in the course of the interview
- Ethics in the writing up of your interviews
- The ethics of care

WHY ETHICS?

There have been periods in human history where what was called 'research' was conducted in an extremely crude and inhumane fashion. This 'research' mainly involved transgressions of the human body without the person's consent. A notorious example is the Tuskegee syphilis study conducted between 1932 and 1972 in Alabama in the United States. Researchers promised the 399 African

American men infected with syphilis (there was a control group of 201 men) that they would receive treatment but this never occurred. At the start of the project in 1932, Dr Taliaferro Clark of the United States Public Health Service commented, 'the Alabama community offered an unparalleled opportunity for the study of the effect of untreated syphilis' (in Jones, 1981: 94). The men were tracked until they died.

The most grotesque and barbaric examples of unethical research are the experiments carried out on prisoners in the name of medical science in extermination camps in Nazi Germany (Berger, 1990; Spitz, 2005). A notorious experiment was the hypothermia experiment that involved immersing prisoners in icy water for extended periods to see how they would respond. Of course there was no voluntary consent, although some prisoners were told that if they participated they would receive certain privileges. Many died during immersion or shortly thereafter (Berger, 1990). A moral and ethical question is whether the results of the experiments should have been used subsequently. Remarkably, by 1984, 45 peer-reviewed publications had drawn on the results of the Nazis' immersion experiments (Berger, 1990: 1435). Other experiments in the extermination camps included injecting prisoners with malaria contaminated blood; forced amputations and transplants; gassing prisoners with mustard gas and purposefully exposing them to the jaundice virus (Spitz, 2005).

Josef Mengele, a medical doctor, besides being centrally involved in deciding who of the new arrivals at the Auschwitz extermination camp should go straight to the gas chambers, conducted horrific experiments on identical twins. His research on over 1000 twins involved the extraction of tissue, muscle and bone often after he had murdered the victims. When Auschwitz was liberated in 1945 only 200 twins were still alive (Müller-Hill, 2001).

In an endeavour to ensure that this total disregard for the welfare of human beings in the name of research never occurs again, the Nuremberg Code was passed in 1947, and in 1964 the Helsinki Declaration, which builds on the Nuremberg Code, was signed by the World Medical Association (Marzano, 2012). Both set out the principles required for conducting ethical research. The first point of the Nuremberg Code declares, 'The voluntary consent of the human subject is absolutely essential' (in Schuster, 1997). Subsequently, the research ethics that govern biomedicine have been incorporated into social research.

The emergence of the expert panel to oversee the granting of permission to proceed with qualitative research has provoked much debate (Haggerty, 2004; Wynn, 2011). Some scholars have argued that qualitative research does not require such strict controls as rarely does it do harm and, if it does, it is usually not serious and is reversible (Gabb, 2010; Hammersley, 2009). Ryen (2012: 482) concludes, 'The auditing model interferes with both research practice and our efforts to produce new knowledge …' She contrasts the onerous demands placed on social scientists with the minimal demands placed on journalists. The relative freedom of journalists in relation to ethics scrutiny when compared with academics is noteworthy especially when you consider the power of the media to shape public opinion and influence elections (Haggerty, 2004: 395). Notwithstanding the importance of this debate, the reality is that a social researcher who wants to conduct interviews needs to apply for ethics clearance from their institution's Ethics committee before they can proceed with their research.[1] Also the ethics application process and review does force the researcher/s to reflect on their methodology and ensure that risk is minimised.

THE KEY PRINCIPLES AND PROCEDURES FOR CONDUCTING RESEARCH ETHICALLY

In many countries, federal law requires institutional compliance and there are national bodies that communicate directives as to how to conduct ethical research. For example, in the United Kingdom, the latest framework for research ethics issued by The Economic and Social Research Council (ESRC)[2] sets out the following six key principles and minimum requirements that need to be adhered to when conducting research:

1. Research should be designed, reviewed and undertaken to ensure integrity, quality and transparency.
2. Research staff and participants must normally be informed fully about the purpose, methods and intended possible uses of the research, what their participation in the research entails and what risks, if any, are involved. Some variation is allowed in very specific research contexts.
3. The confidentiality of information supplied by research participants and the anonymity of respondents must be respected.
4. Research participants must take part voluntarily, free from any coercion.
5. Harm to research participants and researchers must be avoided in all instances.
6. The independence of research must be clear, and any conflicts of interest or partiality must be explicit.

Each principle is elaborated on below.

---

[1] I have used the term Ethics committee rather than Institutional Review Boards (IRBs). The latter term is only used in the United States.

[2] The ESRC guidelines are very similar to those that pertain in the United States, Australia, Canada and elsewhere.

1. Research should be designed, reviewed and undertaken to ensure integrity, quality and transparency

From the outset the researcher should ensure that the research is conducted with total integrity. This implies that there should be no misleading of interviewees and in the reporting of the interviews every endeavour should be made to ensure that the reporting and analysis reflect the data as accurately as possible. In the case of studies reliant on in-depth interviewing this can be challenging, as the analysis will necessarily involve selecting and emphasising some quotes and disregarding others. There is a presumption that what you include and omit should reflect the 'reality' you have been exploring. The quotes should capture the general trends. You should explain to interviewees that the interview material will be used selectively. Ultimately the writing up of interviews is a construction of social reality. You are making choices as to what to include and what to omit; what to emphasise and what not. However, there is an implicit presumption that you do this with integrity (Pitchforth et al., 2005).

2. Research staff and participants must normally be informed fully about the purpose, methods and intended possible uses of the research, what their participation in the research entails and what risks, if any, are involved

Informed consent is crucial. If you conduct an interview and have not obtained informed consent it can have serious implications. If the interviewee makes a formal complaint on the basis that they were not fully informed about the study, you could face disciplinary action from your institution. For example, Columbia University's ethics guidelines for research on human subjects state,

> Federal regulations require that research on human subjects must include a prior review of the project by an IRB [Institutional Review Board]. Any instances of non-compliance must be reported to the appropriate governing agencies. The University's policy states that non-compliance may result in, among other things, suspension or termination of the study; and/or suspension of research privileges at the University. (Columbia University, 2014)

Informed consent requires that interviewees know what the research is about, what the interview will involve and whether there are any risks. A potential interviewee, if they have all the information, should have the capacity to decide whether participating in the research will cause distress.

My one experience with a failure to obtain ethics approval involved a PhD student who I took over as supervisor after his earlier supervisors had retired.

He had been registered for many years and by the time I became his supervisor he had completed all his primary research and was in the process of writing up the final draft. The thesis was duly submitted and one of the examiners noted in his report that there was no mention of ethics approval for the study. On investigation it transpired that due to a lack of knowledge of the requirements and his supervisors failing to inform him, the student had never applied for ethics approval. The consequences were dramatic. The Ethics committee instructed the student to remove all of the interview material in his thesis. Fortunately, the thesis had enough data from other sources (mainly archival), and the revised thesis ultimately passed.

The nature of the project and the profile of the interviewees play a role in determining whether obtaining consent from interviewees is potentially an issue. If you are doing a study that involves research in communities with high levels of illiteracy, the endeavour to obtain written consent could create tension between the interviewer and interviewee (Marzano, 2012). In countries with a colonial past, interviewees could be wary about signing the consent form: 'In many cultural settings, signing a form is not an innocuous and routine act, for it evokes painful memories of colonial abuses or governmental injustices' (Marzano, 2012: 445). There is little doubt that historically a great deal of research on Indigenous people has been exploitative and has focused on supposed deficiencies in Indigenous communities rather than its strengths (Ermine et al., 2004). In Australia, a report commissioned by the Northern Territory government into sexual abuse of Aboriginal children (Wild and Anderson, 2007), was used by the federal government to justify what was called the Northern Territory Intervention. The intervention involved a dramatic tightening up of how Aboriginal people in the Northern Territory could spend welfare payments and imposed a range of restrictions that only applied to Aboriginal communities. The restrictions were presented as essential elements of the fight against child sexual abuse. The authors of the report have alleged that their findings have been totally misused by the federal government (Cresswell, 2011).

3. The confidentiality of information supplied by research participants and the anonymity of respondents must be respected

Confidentiality and anonymity are fundamental components of ethical research. In the writing up of interview material it is essential that the interviewee not be identified: 'Nothing reported from the study, in print or in lecture, should permit identification of respondents' (Weiss, 1994: 131). Maintaining confidentiality is usually not difficult but in certain circumstances it can be challenging. There are occasions when the circumstances of the interviewee are so specific that it is difficult to 'deidentify' them. However, even in these circumstances, it is imperative that every attempt is made to ensure confidentiality. This may mean that you do not divulge details like the person's age, city and occupation. Alternatively, if it is likely that in the reporting of the research it is possible that the interviewee could be identified, it is essential that this possibility be discussed with the participant. One possibility is to discuss the findings with interviewees so as to ascertain whether they feel comfortable with the way they are portrayed (Heggen and Guillemin, 2012: 468).

An in-depth examination of a small bounded community does risk exposing the identities of individuals even if pseudonyms are used and, in a context where most people know one another, this can have ramifications. Carolyn Ellis (2007) recounts the difficulties of maintaining anonymity when doing qualitative research in a small community. Many of the characters in her book on a small fishing village were identifiable, despite the use of pseudonyms.

> My strategy of inventing pseudonyms starting with the same letters as the double names of the Fishneckers had made it easy for them. However, even without these clues, they recognised the stories they had told me and themselves as the characters. (Ellis, 2007: 11)

Several years after the publication of her research she returned to find that many of the people who had participated in her study were angry and felt betrayed by her unflattering portrayal of the residents. Their anger is not surprising:

> … they reacted strongly to my description of their smelling like fish, taking infrequent baths, being overweight, making little money, wearing mismatched clothing, having sex at an early age, and being uneducated. (Ellis, 2007: 11)

Confidentiality and anonymity also requires that the in-depth interview transcripts are securely stored. Usually a locked filing cabinet is adequate. With the advent of digital voice recorders the storage of audio-tapes is no longer an issue. However Aldridge and Medina (2008: 2) make the important point that we need 'to recognise that digitally held data does not automatically provide for "better" security', rather it brings new challenges around security. Inspired by the theft of a laptop storing digital data collected from interviews, they have developed a useful set of guidelines for securing digital data. They argue that paper print-outs of data should be minimised and all data should be anonymised as soon as possible and that passwords used to protect access to computers/laptops should be complex. They argue that the average password is easily bypassed and that ideally you should use 'encryption software to provide secure places to hold data on desktop and laptop computers, and on portable storage media such as memory sticks' (Aldridge and Medina, 2008: 4). The use of encryption software to store interview data is not common and few Ethics committees require it. If your interview material is sensitive (Aldridge and Medina had been interviewing gang members about their associates and criminal acts), then it is recommended that you discuss with your institution the storage of your data using encryption software.

4. Research participants must take part voluntarily, free from any coercion

It is imperative that interviewees voluntarily agree that they are prepared to be interviewed. This principle overlaps with research integrity and informed consent in that interviewees need to be fully informed so as to ensure that their decision to participate is voluntary. Paying interviewees is now a common practice and an interesting question is whether payment for interviews can undermine the notion of voluntary participation. Do people participate not because they want to, but because they need the monetary reward? Clearly, if the payment offered is excessive there is a danger of people agreeing to be interviewed purely for the financial gain and it could be argued that this does involve a degree of implicit coercion (Goodman et al., 2004). However, it can also be argued that a reasonable payment for participants is fair as you are paying people for their time. Also, in some cases, it is difficult to recruit interviewees if there is no monetary inducement (Head, 2009).

5. Harm to research participants and researchers must be avoided in all instances

There is evidence that in-depth interviews rarely cause serious distress and that in many instances interviewees enjoy the experience and may even find it therapeutic (Corbin and Morse, 2003). However, it is evident that in-depth interviewing is an intrusive research method. You are asking a person to discuss personal 'stuff' and, in some cases, there is a possibility that the interview could produce distress. What will happen in an interview situation is unpredictable and the potential risks are not necessarily known at the beginning of the research. In a study of adolescent girls diagnosed with anorexia nervosa, Halse and Honey (2005: 2150) were concerned that 'the interviews might revive distressing, secreted trauma'. In studies where interviews could cause distress, the researcher is expected to have guidelines in place as to how they will deal with this occurrence.

The issue of possible harm is most pertinent when dealing with vulnerable groups such as children, people with a disability, people with serious or terminal illnesses or oppressed minority groups. Any research on what is deemed a vulnerable group will be closely scrutinised by the Ethics committee. Obtaining ethics clearance for research on vulnerable groups is certainly possible, but the process, depending on the nature of the research, may be lengthy and complex. There is a well founded belief that these groups are more susceptible to harm and that the steps in place to deal with distress during the interview should be clear.

Thus research on children invariably requires a more rigorous ethics process. In Australia, The National Statement on Ethical Conduct in Human Research (2014: 50) comments that research involving children raises particular ethical concerns about 'Their capacity to understand what the research entails, and therefore whether their consent to participate is sufficient for their participation.' It concludes that in their research design it is incumbent on the researchers to 'specify how they will judge the child's vulnerability and capacity to consent to participation in research.' There are instances where the child can consent to be involved in the research without the additional consent of a parent or guardian. The National Statement (2014) states,

> An ethical review body may approve research to which only the young person consents if it is satisfied that he or she is mature enough to understand and consent, and not vulnerable through immaturity in ways that would warrant additional consent from a parent or guardian. (2014: 51)

If you want to conduct interviews in schools, in most contexts you will have to obtain ethics approval from the relevant educational authority and your institution.

Another vulnerable group is refugees. Pittaway et al. (2010: 231), in a discussion of the ethics of research on these groups, conclude 'the ethical challenge is for researchers to add value to the lives of the people they are researching, recognizing them as subjects in the process and not simply as sources of data.'

Research on disabled people can also present complex ethical challenges. It has been argued that historically research on people with intellectual disabilities has 'often dehumanised them as psycho-medical curiosities or freaks' (Dowse, 2009: 142). The National Statement (2014) states that,

> People with a cognitive impairment, an intellectual disability, or a mental illness are entitled to participate in research … [however] The capacity of a person with any of these conditions to consent to research, and the ability to participate in it, can vary, for many reasons … (2014: 58)

A key issue is that people with these conditions may be more vulnerable to stress and discomfort. As such, extra care needs to be taken to ensure that the possibility of distress is minimised.

Interviewing vulnerable groups can be beneficial for interviewees. For example, in a study of the relationships of terminally ill patients with their nurses, Raudonis (1992: 242) recalls how an interviewee expressed her delight at being able to participate as rather than being helped it gave her a chance to help people, something she could no longer do.

A major ethical concern is research with Indigenous communities. In Australia the National Statement has set out clear guidelines for research with Aboriginal and Torres Strait Islander individuals and communities. It identifies six core values that should be adhered to – reciprocity, respect, equality, responsibility, survival and protection, spirit and integrity. A key requirement is that the research should be supported by the communities concerned and 'engage with their social and cultural practices' (National Statement, 2014: 63). There should be discussion and agreement around recruitment, obtaining consent and reporting back of results and, where possible and appropriate, members of the community should be involved in the actual fieldwork. The research should benefit the community:

> The benefits from research should include the enhancement or establishment of capabilities, opportunities or research outcomes that advance the interests of Aboriginal and Torres Strait Islander Peoples. (National Statement, 2014: 63)

6. The independence of research must be clear, and any conflicts of interest or partiality must be explicit

If you have obtained funding for your research you should acknowledge your sponsor/s when you write up your research. Of course, it is crucial that your sponsor has no role in shaping your data or conclusions. Think tanks, corporations and lobby groups fund a substantial proportion of contemporary research. The impartiality of research that is funded by these groupings is often questionable. A prime example is the pharmaceutical industry. Historically, pharmaceutical companies have been major funders of drug-related research and have been accused of not taking heed of results that could damage a drug's reputation and profitability. In a major review of the relationship between pharmaceutical corporations and clinical trial results, Sismondo (2008: 112) concluded 'Pharmaceutical company funding systematically biases the clinical trials literature in favour of new drugs'. A significant contemporary example of research being influenced by sponsors is climate change research. Research funded by conservative think tanks invariably questions the science of climate change (McCright and Dunlap, 2010).

APPLYING FOR ETHICS APPROVAL FROM YOUR INSTITUTION'S ETHICS COMMITTEE AND THE DECISION-MAKING PROCESS

The usual procedure is that there is a designated ethics application form that the researcher has to complete and send to the relevant Ethics committee. You should not do any interviews until you have obtained ethics approval. The application form usually has standard requests. Most require that you provide a summary of the project; outline the methodology; discuss how interviewees will be recruited and whether they will be reimbursed; affirm whether the interviews could cause distress and, if so, how this will be dealt with. Usually you need to explain how the confidentiality of the data will be ensured. You are expected to attach an information sheet, consent form and an interview guide. Of course, the interview guide for semi-structured interviews is flexible. As Halse and Honey (2005: 2148) observe, '... semi-structured interviews are inherently emergent, reflexive, and messy, and the planned focus of an interview can easily shift as new issues and accounts emerge.'

If your study has minimal risk, obtaining ethics approval is generally straightforward. For example, it is likely that a study that examined alternative food and masculinities using in-depth interviews (Nath, 2011) did not elicit much concern within the relevant Ethics committee. The ethics committee will want to be sure that the questions you propose to ask are reasonable, will not provoke undue distress, that the proposed method for recruiting participants is sensible, the information sheet is clear and there is full disclosure.

The most common reasons for an ethics application where the primary or sole method is in-depth interviews not being approved first time round, is a perception that the interviews may cause distress and a lack of clarity as to what the researcher will do if the interviewee becomes distressed; you need to have details of a counselling service to which you can refer interviewees.

If the planned study is deemed potentially risky for the researcher, the Ethics committee is likely to request safeguards so as to ensure that you and the interviewees are protected. If, for example, you are wanting to do a study of what motivates people to join gangs, the committee will carefully scrutinise how you intend to do the study. It has a duty of care to ensure that in the course of doing your research you do not put yourself in any danger. There is a possibility that the committee may conclude that the intended project is too dangerous and may not approve your application or alternatively demand substantial changes so as to minimise the risk.

The ethics approval process has the potential to have significant ramifications for your research. If you have limited time and resources it is probably not a good idea to pursue a project that the Ethics committee is likely to view as high risk. The proposed study may not be approved or alternatively the approval process could be difficult and lengthy and put you under time pressure.

The information sheet

The information sheet is part of the consent form and is an essential component of informed consent. It should tell the participant who is doing the research what the research is about; what the research will involve; whether there are any risks attached; why the person has been invited to be part of the research; that information relayed by participants will remain confidential (this can be in the consent form); that they can withdraw from the research at any time and if there are any concerns or complaints participants are encouraged to talk to the researcher or the Research Ethics Office of the institution to which the researcher is affiliated.

Before beginning the interview, the interviewee needs to be given the chance to read the Information Sheet or alternatively you can go through it with them. It is essential that the interviewee understands the nature and purpose of the research and the ramifications of agreeing to participate. The risks and benefits of the study should be made clear. Usually understanding the Information Sheet is not an issue. However, in the case of interviewees whose English is poor or who are not literate, it is potentially challenging. Ideally, the Information Sheet should be short, precise and unintimidating and you should avoid academic terms. Figure 2.1 below provides an example.

INFORMATION SHEET
The impact of housing tenure on the lives of people who are dependent primarily on the age pension for their income (approval number ....)

WHO IS DOING THE RESEARCH?

My name is Alan Morris and I am an academic at UTS.

WHAT IS THIS RESEARCH ABOUT?

This research is to find out about how the housing tenure you reside in (private rental, public/community housing, manufactured homes or homeownership) influences your everyday life and financial status. The purpose of the research is to understand the impact of housing tenure and to make recommendations to policy-makers based on the research.

IF I SAY YES, WHAT WILL IT INVOLVE?

If you say yes to participating in the research I will ask you to participate in an in-depth interview. This should not take longer than 50 minutes to complete and with your consent will be audio-recorded.

ARE THERE ANY RISKS/INCONVENIENCE?

There are very few if any risks because the research has been carefully designed. However, it is possible that you could find a couple of the questions uncomfortable and/or embarrassing.

(Continued)

WHY HAVE I BEEN ASKED?

You are able to give me the information I need to find out about because you are primarily or solely dependent on the age pension for your income.

DO I HAVE TO SAY YES? WHAT WILL HAPPEN IF I SAY NO?

You don't have to say yes to participating, and if you say no there are no consequences and you will not be contacted again about this research.

IF I SAY YES, CAN I CHANGE MY MIND LATER?

You can change your mind at any time and you don't have to say why. I will thank you for your time so far and won't contact you about this research again.

WHAT IF I HAVE CONCERNS OR A COMPLAINT?

If you have concerns about the research that you think I can help you with, please feel free to contact me on …………

If you would like to talk to someone who is not connected with the research, you may contact the Research Ethics Officer on …………, and quote this number …………

Figure 2.1 *Example of an Information Sheet*

The consent form

The consent form varies in style from institution to institution. For an example, see Figure 2.2 below. It usually reiterates what the study is about; why the person has been selected; states that the research is confidential and that interviewees will be deidentified when the research is written up. The interviewee needs to sign the consent form prior to you starting the formal interview.

CONSENT FORM

I _____ agree to participate in the research project 'The impact of housing tenure on the lives of people who are dependent primarily on the age pension for their income', approval number (…………) being conducted by Alan Morris, Centre for Local Government, UTS, PO Box 123, Broadway, 2700, telephone …………

I understand that the purpose of this study is to learn how the housing tenure I reside in (private rental, public/community housing, manufactured home or homeownership) influences my everyday life and financial status.

I understand that I have been asked to participate in this research because I am primarily or solely dependent on the age pension and that my participation in this research will involve participation in an in-depth interview that should not take longer than 50 minutes to complete and I can withdraw from the research at any time and without giving a reason. All the information I provide will remain totally confidential. In the reporting of the interview I will not be identified.

I am aware that I can contact Alan Morris if I have any concerns about the research. I also understand that I may refuse to answer any questions and am free to withdraw my participation from this research project at any time I wish, without consequences, and without giving a reason.

I agree that Alan Morris has answered all my questions fully and clearly.

I agree that the research data gathered from this project may be published in a form that identifies me/does not identify me in any way.

_____   ____/____/____

Signature (participant)

_____   ____/____/____

Signature (researcher or delegate)

NOTE:

This study has been approved by the University of Technology, Sydney Human Research Ethics committee. If you have any complaints or reservations about any aspect of your participation in this research which you cannot resolve with the researcher, you may contact the ethics committee through the Research Ethics Officer (ph.: ………… email: …………), and quote the UTS HREC reference number. Any complaint you make will be treated in confidence and investigated fully and you will be informed of the outcome.

Figure 2.2 *Example of a consent form*

RESPONDING TO AN INITIAL REQUEST FROM THE ETHICS COMMITTEE FOR CLARIFICATION

In my experience Ethics committees rarely grant ethics approval the first time around. Typically, applicants will be asked to supply additional information. The number and complexity of the requests made by the Ethics committee will depend on the quality of the application and the perceived level of risk. It will also depend on the level of support the applicant was able to obtain from the ethics office in their institution prior to submitting the application. Some institutions have staff that will give you expert guidance and help eliminate any potential problems before submission. Below is a typical Ethics committee response. The application was for a low-risk topic – the primary aim of the study was to examine how housing tenure shapes the lives of older people who are primarily or solely dependent on the government age pension for their income.

From: University Ethics committee
To: Alan Morris

Dear Alan,

Thank you for your application to the HREA Panel B. Before the Panel can recommend your application for approval to the Deputy Vice Chancellor Research, they have asked that you please address the following:

Q4: Will there be any remuneration for participants and the offering of their time? This is of particular concern given the possibility that participants may be of vulnerable financial status.

Q5: Explain what the statement of minimal distress is based on; expand on this further with reference to your previous experience or expertise and how this will help you alleviate any stress and minimise any risk and/or harm.

Q5: Will you have any other systems in place to comfort participants? That is, stopping the interview, having a break, etc.

Q6: Provide further details on recruitment – where will posters be displayed? For example, Centrelink? Via which services will recruitment occur?

Q6: Where will participants be asked to travel? Would it be possible to travel to them to minimise inconvenience?

Q9: Will transcripts be read to participants or provided for reading/checking?

Q9: What type of recording device will be used? Will this be unobtrusive?

IS (Information sheet): Include page numbers (i.e., 1 of 2, 2 of 2).

IS: Project titles do not match the title provided at Q3; please amend to correct title.

IS: Provide on the appropriate School letterhead.

IS: State in paragraph one your name, your status as a researcher, the purpose of the research and the school and institution you are from.

IS: State the reason the participant has been selected.

IS: Include sentence informing participants they can stop the interview at any time.

Please make all changes to your application in a single electronic file and forward the revised application to me. There is no need to supply hard copies.

Please do not send back your amended application without carefully addressing all the Panel's comments. If all comments are not addressed, your application will be returned to you.

All changes to your application must be highlighted. Please include page numbers and indicate on what pages the requested changes have been made.

The requests are fairly straightforward. The most complex request is the request for more information on how distress will be minimised. In my original submission I had written, 'There is a very small possibility that an interviewee could find some of the questions posed unsettling. I would say the potential for psychological harm is very minimal. If an interviewee does suffer any distress they will be referred to the Wesley Mission Counselling Service, phone (02) 8963 9020 (Ashfield office) or (02) 9273 5589 (City office).' The Ethics committee wanted more detail on the issue of whether the interviews could provoke distress and how distress would be dealt with. The response below satisfied the Committee:

> There is a very small possibility that an interviewee could find some of the questions posed unsettling. I would say the potential for psychological harm is very minimal. Based on the numerous interviews I have done with older people on this topic, it is safe to conclude that the vast majority of older interviewees enjoy having the opportunity to talk about the issue with somebody who is an outsider but has expertise in the area. Older private renters are the most vulnerable group and there have been instances of very mild distress when they talk about their financial situation.
>
> If an interviewee does suffer any distress they will be referred to the Wesley Mission Counselling Service, phone (02) 8963 9020 (Ashfield office) or (02) 9273 5589 (City office). I will also change topic if the subject under consideration is causing distress. Alternatively, I will take a short break. If the interview is clearly causing distress I will stop the interview.

A key aspect about responding to a request from an Ethics committee is to respond to every concern raised as comprehensively as possible. There is little point being defensive as the committee is unlikely to back down on a concern it has flagged. Of course, if you feel strongly that what the committee is suggesting is problematic or is premised on a misunderstanding, you are entitled to defend your approach.

Some studies involve obtaining ethics approval from more than one institution. As mentioned, in these instances, especially if it is a topic with risk attached, ethics approval can be a challenging and lengthy process. Each of the Ethics committees involved will have their own take on the topic and procedures. If you are planning to conduct interviews in schools or hospitals or prisons you should be prepared for a lengthy process and plan accordingly.

HOW TO PREVENT AND RESPOND TO ETHICAL ISSUES ARISING IN THE COURSE OF THE INTERVIEW

There is always the possibility that in the course of doing your research you may transgress what is viewed as ethical behaviour. It is thus important to have a good understanding of what is appropriate and what is not appropriate in the interview situation. Guillemin and Gillam (2004) use the term 'ethical mindfulness' to capture the dynamics of ethical behaviour during the interview. A central feature of ethical mindfulness is that the researcher be aware of 'ethically important moments'. These refer to subtle indications that the interviewee is feeling stressed.

What is important is that you are prepared for the possibility that the interview does not necessarily go smoothly. In the course of the interview you have to make judgement calls. An in-depth interview can become deeply personal and the researcher has to decide instantly if they should pursue a particular angle. For example, if the participant is an older person who is retired, it may emerge that since their partner died they have been desperately lonely and only leave their home to go shopping. This may be the first time the interviewee has told anybody about their isolation, and in the course of revealing this they may become deeply distressed. You can decide to push on and ask what impact being so lonely has had and whether they see this as temporary. Alternatively, you could offer some comfort and move on to a different topic. You need to assess whether pursuing the interview could result in the interviewee suffering further distress. Abruptly changing topic could be interpreted as a cold and inappropriate response.

If the topic and line of questioning is clearly upsetting the interviewee it is important that you take stock of the situation immediately. It may be appropriate to stop the interview and ask the interviewee if they are okay and whether they want to continue the interview. You could also ask if they would like the contact details of a counselling service; you should have the telephone number at hand.

If you persist in pursuing a topic that is causing distress, the interviewee may have grounds to lay a formal complaint with the Ethics Office of your institution.

A particularly difficult issue but one you are fortunately unlikely to experience, is the disclosure of illegal activity by the interviewee. In these instances you should discuss the disclosure with your supervisor or manager and decide on an appropriate course of action.

ETHICS IN THE WRITING UP OF YOUR INTERVIEWS

Confidentiality

As mentioned, a fundamental expectation is that the confidentiality of interviewees is not breached. If you think that in the writing up of the interviews there is a possibility that an interviewee could be identified but that publication of the information is essential for the analysis, you need to ask their permission to publish the material in question. Another option, which is less common and could have unintended consequences, is to show interviewees the write-up of the research before publication. They are then given the opportunity to veto what they see as misrepresentation, revelations which they view as potentially damaging or descriptions which have the potential to identify participants. This process can have advantages. It allows interviewees to check the accuracy of the data and allows you to conduct and publish research which may not have been possible without this agreement (Kaiser, 2012: 464). There are rare instances when the interviewee may insist that their actual name is used when the research is written up. They may want their voices to be heard (Kaiser, 2012).

Accurate representation

A more amorphous ethical issue is the way you write up your data. You have an ethical responsibility to ensure that the write-up captures the narratives of the interviewees and does not distort their responses. It is a difficult balance as you have the ultimate power to select what data you feel are relevant and if you have done a substantial number of interviews there is no doubt that a sizeable proportion of the interview material collected will have to be omitted from the final write-up. This may upset some interviewees. However, ultimately it is your work and as long as you feel that 'the reality' under review has been accurately presented, this should forestall any ethical issues.

It is important that if the interviews are being transcribed that the transcriber not change the words of participants. It is not ethical to misrepresent the responses of interviewees.

THE ETHICS OF CARE

Some scholars have argued that the researcher has a constant obligation to the research participants and that your relationship does not end when the interview is complete.

> … an ethics of care means involving the participants in the write-up of the research work or asking for their approval of the final text, caring about their general welfare, supporting their causes, being interested in their empowerment, and considering the potential benefits to them of participation in the research. (Marzano, 2012: 451)

This approach is especially pertinent when your research has been on groups that historically have been marginalised and oppressed. Thus, if you have been examining the lives of Indigenous Australians who were removed from their parents (the 'stolen generation'), an ethics of care may involve following up on interviewees who are in particularly vulnerable situations and asking them if they would like to be put in touch with a counselling service. It may also involve publicising their plight outside of the academy.

The questions you ask can have an impact on the interviewee and it is your responsibility to ensure that the power you have as the interviewer is used wisely.

SUMMARY

The chapter first discusses how the establishment of ethical protocols for research was driven by the determination of the world community to ensure that inhumane and callous research that reached its peak in the extermination camps of the Third Reich is never repeated. The chapter then discusses the six ethical principles identified by the Economic and Social Research Council (ESRC) in the United Kingdom that need to be adhered to if research is to be conducted in an ethical fashion. The fundamental components of ethical research are that there should be full transparency; participation should be totally voluntary; if at all possible participants should not suffer any harm; confidentiality should be assured; and the research should be independent. The process of applying for ethics is then discussed. Examples are given of an information sheet and consent form. Both forms need to be precise and easy to read and contain all relevant information. An example of how to respond to an Ethics committee's initial seeking of clarification prior to giving ethics approval is then discussed. All the points raised by the Ethics committee have to be taken on board. The ethical issues that can emerge while conducting an interview are discussed. The Guillemin and Gillam (2004) term, 'ethical mindfulness', is used as a guide. The interviewer needs to be constantly aware of the possibility that the interviewee may experience distress and needs to respond appropriately if the distress becomes significant. The ethical concerns in the writing up of interviews, mainly confidentiality and accuracy of representation, are also examined. The chapter closes with a discussion of the 'ethics of care' – the notion that your responsibility to interviewees, especially if they are from vulnerable groups, does not end when you have completed the interview. It may involve advocacy and publicising of their situation and concern about their general welfare.

Exercise

Construct an Information Sheet for two of the topics listed below. Include a section on how you will ensure that distress is minimised and what you will do if interviewees do experience distress. You should also discuss how you will minimise risk.

- Gang members
- Homeless youth
- Sex workers
- Children who have been bullied at school
- Refugees who have endured torture
- Precarious workers who cannot speak English

REFERENCES

Aldridge, J. and Medina, J. (2008) *Improving the Security of Qualitative Data in a Digital Age: A Protocol for Researchers.* Manchester: University of Manchester.

Berger, R.L. (1990) 'Nazi science – the Dachau hypothermia experiments', *The New England Journal of Medicine*, 322 (20): 1435–40.

Columbia University (2014) 'Research compliance and administration system: frequently asked questions: human subjects'. New York: Columbia University. Available at: https://www.rascal.columbia.edu/help/irbfaq.html#qd5, accessed 9 August 2014.

Corbin, J. and Morse, J.M. (2003) 'The unstructured interactive interview: issues of reciprocity and risks when dealing with sensitive topics', *Qualitative Inquiry*, 9 (3): 335–54.

Cresswell, A. (2011) 'Intervention "based on ignorance": Anderson', *The Australian*, 6 May.

Dowse, L. (2009) It's like being in a zoo: researching with people with intellectual disability', *Journal of Research in Special Educational Needs*, 9 (3): 141–53.

Ellis, C. (2007) 'Telling secrets, revealing lives', *Qualitative Inquiry*, 13 (1): 3–29.

Ermine, W., Sinclair, R., Jeffery, B. and Saskatoon, S.K. (2004) *The Ethics of Research Involving Indigenous Peoples*. Regina, Saskatchewan: Indigenous Peoples' Health Research Centre.

Gabb, J. (2010) 'Home truths. Ethical issues in family research', *Qualitative Research*, 10 (4): 461–78.

Goodman, L.A., Liang, B., Helms, J.E., Latta, R.E., Sparks, E. and Weintraub, S.R. (2004) 'Training counselling psychologists as social justice agents: feminist and multicultural principles in action', *Counselling Psychologist*, 32 (6): 793–837.

Guillemin, M. and Gillam, L. (2004) 'Ethics, reflexivity and "ethically important moments" in research', *Qualitative Inquiry*, 10 (2): 261–80.

Haggerty, K.D. (2004) 'Ethics creep: governing social science research in the name of ethics', *Qualitative Sociology*, 27 (4): 391–414.

Halse, C. and Honey, A. (2005) 'Unraveling ethics: illuminating the moral dilemmas of research ethics', *Signs*, 30 (4): 2141–62.

Hammersley, M. (2009) 'Against the ethicists: on the evils of ethical regulation', *International Journal of Social Research Methodology*, 12 (3): 211–25.

Head, E. (2009) 'The ethics and implications of paying participants in qualitative research', *International Journal of Social Research Methodology*, 12 (4): 335–44.

Heggen, K. and Guillemin, M. (2012) 'Protecting participants' confidentiality using a situated research ethics approach', in J.F. Gubrium, J.A. Holstein, A.B. Marvasti and K.D. McKinney (eds), *The SAGE Handbook of Interview Research: The Complexity of the Craft*. Thousand Oaks, CA: SAGE Publications. pp. 465–77.

Jones, J. (1981) *Bad Blood: The Tuskegee Syphilis Experiment – A Tragedy of Race and Medicine*. New York, NY: The Free Press.

Kaiser, K. (2012) 'Protecting confidentiality', in J.F. Gubrium, J.A. Holstein, A.B. Marvasti and K.D. McKinney (eds), *The SAGE Handbook of Interview Research: The Complexity of the Craft*. Thousand Oaks, CA: SAGE Publications. pp. 457–65.

Marzano, M. (2012) 'Informed consent', in J.F. Gubrium, J.A. Holstein, A.B. Marvasti and K.D. McKinney (eds), *The SAGE Handbook of Interview Research: The Complexity of the Craft*. Thousand Oaks, CA: SAGE Publications. pp. 443–57.

McCright, A.M. and Dunlap, R.E. (2010) 'Anti-Reflexivity: The American Conservative Movement's Success in Undermining Climate Science and Policy', *Theory, Culture and Society*, 27 (2–3): 100–33.

Müller-Hill, B. (2001) 'Genetics of susceptibility to tuberculosis: Mengele's experiments in Auschwitz', *Nature Reviews/Genetics*, 2 (August): 631–3.

Nath, J. (2011) Gendered fare? A qualitative study of alternative food and masculinities, *Journal of Sociology*, 47 (3): 261–78.

National Statement on Ethical Conduct in Human Research 2007 (Updated March 2014) The National Health and Medical Research Council, the Australian Research Council and the Australian Vice-Chancellors' Committee. Canberra: Commonwealth of Australia.

Pitchforth, E., Porter, M., van Teijlingen, E. and Forrest Keenan, K. (2005) 'Writing up and presenting qualitative research in family planning and reproductive health care', *The Journal of Family Planning and Reproductive Health Care*, 31 (2): 132–5.

Pittaway, E., Bartolomei, L. and Hugman, R. (2010) '"Stop stealing our stories": the ethics of research with vulnerable groups', *Journal of Human Rights Practice*, 2 (2): 229–51.

Raudonis, B.M. (1992) 'Ethical considerations in qualitative research with hospice patients', *Qualitative Health Research*, 2 (2): 238–49.

Ryen, A. (2012) 'Assessing the risk of being interviewed', in J.F. Gubrium, J.A. Holstein, A.B. Marvasti and K.D. McKinney (eds), *The SAGE Handbook of Interview Research: The Complexity of the Craft*. Thousand Oaks, CA: SAGE Publications. pp. 477–95.

Schuster, E. (1997) 'Fifty years later: the significance of the Nuremberg Code', *The New England Journal of Medicine*, 337: 1436–40.

Sismondo, S. (2008) 'Pharmaceutical company funding and its consequences: a qualitative systematic review', *Contemporary Clinical Trials*, 29 (2): 109–13.

Spitz, V. (2005) *Doctors from Hell: The Horrific Account of Nazi Experiments on Humans*. Boulder, Colorado: Sentient Publications.

Weiss, R.S. (1994) *Learning from Strangers: The Art and Method of Qualitative Interview Studies*. New York: Free Press.

Wild, R. and Anderson, P. (2007) *Ampe Akelyernemane Meke Mekarle: Little Children are Sacred*. Report of the Northern Territory Board of Inquiry into the Protection of Aboriginal Children from Sexual Abuse. Darwin: Northern Territory Government.

Wynn, L.L. (2011) 'Ethnographers' experience of institutional ethics oversight: results from a quantitative and qualitative survey', *Journal of Policy History*, 23 (1): 94–114.

3

DEVELOPING THE INTERVIEW GUIDE

Developing an effective interview guide is central to the conducting of a semi-structured in-depth interview. Although the semi-structured interview gives you the scope to digress and talk about unexpected aspects, all the major topics in the interview guide should ultimately be covered. The data elicited from the questions should give you the capacity to answer the research questions you are investigating. Chapter headings include:

- Things to do prior to constructing the interview guide
- The research question
- Constructing the interview guide – key topics or themes
- Questions within topics
- Ordering the themes and questions
- What questions not to ask

THINGS TO DO PRIOR TO CONSTRUCTING THE INTERVIEW GUIDE

An interview guide is essential for focusing the research. It details the main themes or topics and the questions that the researcher wants to ask. The level of detail can vary considerably and to some extent it depends on your approach. A researcher using a 'realist approach' is likely to have a far more detailed interview guide than somebody using a life history or narrative approach. There is a danger that if your interview guide is too detailed and you are intent on sticking to it, you may limit the capacity of the interviewee to make important digressions and reveal significant detail. Alternatively, if your interview guide is too sparse you may fail to cover important topics (King and Horrocks, 2012: 36). What is key is to ensure that all topics that you want to cover are covered, but to keep in mind that your guide is merely a guide and that you give the interviewee the scope to digress and do not treat the interview guide as a prescribed script.

Prior to constructing the interview guide you should have a clear idea of your topic and research question/s (what exactly is a research question is discussed in the following section). As Flick (2004: 149) observes, 'the research question of a qualitative investigation is one of the decisive factors in its success or failure'. Of course, one of the key advantages of qualitative research is that you are able to adjust your research focus and add new questions at any time (King and Horrocks, 2012). Nevertheless, before you start interviewing you should have a well defined idea of the research question/s you are trying to answer. If you fail to ask an important question in the interviews, it is usually difficult to go back to the people already interviewed.

Although it is common to have a fair amount of anecdotal knowledge, preparation of the interview guide requires that you familiarise yourself with existing research on the topic. This will help you formulate your research questions and the interview guide. It will also clarify what are the gaps in the existing research. The more knowledge you have of the area, the greater the likelihood that your research questions will be appropriate and the questions you ask in the interview will generate the data required.

For some topics a useful preparatory strategy is to talk to key stakeholders and discuss your draft interview guide with them. People who have worked in the area under investigation are bound to have useful knowledge and insights and could make an important contribution. For example, if you are investigating the impact that accessing secure housing with support has on the quality of life of people with mental illness (Muir et al., 2008), it would be useful to speak to the professionals who were involved with establishing the programme before interviewing the clients.

THE RESEARCH QUESTION

Your overall topic and the research question guide what you will ask in the interview. The research question is the mystery you are going to try and answer. If you are investigating young people of Pakistani descent in the United Kingdom, your research question could be, 'how do they view themselves and what contributes to their sense of identity?' (see Mythen, 2012). The research question in a study of homeless youth in Melbourne, Australia was, 'how does the experience of homelessness impact on the subjectivity of the people affected?' or to express it another way, 'How do they see themselves?' (Farrugia, 2010). You could have a number of research questions. In my study of inner-city transition in Johannesburg, I had several research questions: Why did the white residents move out of the area? Why did black people move into the area despite racist legislation that made living in the area a criminal offence? Why did the apartheid government allow their 'sacred' policy of racial segregation/apartheid to disintegrate so dramatically in the inner city of Johannesburg? Why did certain apartment blocks decline significantly while others remained in reasonable or pristine condition? Why was crime so high in the area? These were the key research questions explored.

The questions you ask interviewees should help you answer your research questions. However, one of the strengths of semi-structured in-depth interviewing as a method is that it gives you flexibility. It is likely that as the research progresses questions will emerge that you had not thought of at the outset. The proponents of grounded theory argue that as your research progresses, the research questions will emerge and your research question/s should be fairly general at the start of your research (Glaser and Strauss, 1967). This approach has merit but personally I think it is useful to have your research questions formulated when you go out into the field. They help guide the research and give you the basis for constructing your interview guide. Of course, you need to remain open to new possibilities.

CONSTRUCTING THE INTERVIEW GUIDE – KEY TOPICS OR THEMES

The interview guide is constituted by key topics that fundamentally structure the interview. Although the interviewer has a great deal of flexibility when conducting the interview and the interview will take many twists and turns, each topic should be covered. As the research progresses it is likely that certain topics will emerge as central and others will be viewed as less significant.

Deciding on the topics

What is crucial is that the responses to the topics should allow you to collect the data necessary to answer your research question/s and they should resonate with existing research on the overarching topic. For example, if you are examining *the impact of being unemployed and the possibilities of re-entering the workforce*, you need to think through what are the issues and what has existing research established. There is consensus that the experience of unemployment, especially if it is long term, can be debilitating psychologically and materially. In their classic qualitative study on the impacts of unemployment, Jahoda et al. (1971) concluded that besides being impoverishing, unemployment has five major impacts. It takes away shared experience; a structured experience of time; collective purpose; status and identity; and required regular activity. Jahoda et al.'s study could play a key role in shaping your interview guide. Each of their findings could be a sub-theme, the primary theme could be the impact of unemployment, and you could test their conclusions. In relation to shared experience you may ask interviewees how important work was in regards to friendships and whether unemployment has led to a decline in social contact and difficulties in social interaction. This is premised on work giving individuals a common foundation and material for conversation. The impact of not having a temporal structure due to no longer having to go to work, could be a key and interesting theme. Interviewees could be asked how they spend their days and what impact, if any, not having to go to work has. Jahoda et al. saw the lack of a temporal structure regulated by work as necessarily negative and concluded that it fostered depression. You may find that some interviewees find unemployment liberating as it gives them time to engage in pursuits that they find interesting and meaningful. The issue of collective purpose would involve asking questions about what work meant for the interviewees and whether not having employment means that they have little or no purpose in life. The question of status and identity overlaps with collective purpose. You could ask if they feel stigmatised and whether they are treated differently because they are unemployed.

An interesting question is whether work is important for people's identities. The theme of the impact of not having 'required regular activity' overlaps with a lack of temporal structure. The impact of not having regular activity could be interrogated by asking interviewees whether they miss the routine of having to go to work. The notion that regular activity is crucial for well-being has been questioned. For example, Bauman (1998: 7) contends that 'the work ethic was ... about the surrender of freedom'.

In many countries the government benefit paid to people who are unemployed is minimal (see Aleksynska and Schindler, 2011). This potentially has dire implications and a comprehensive analysis of unemployment would focus on the various implications of this minimal support. An important question is whether the minimal income support motivates people to re-enter the labour force or does it serve as an obstacle (Morris and Wilson, 2014). More recent research on unemployment benefits has assessed the effectiveness of employment assistance programmes (Davidson, 2011). This could be an important topic – are the employment assistance programmes, that interviewees are often forced to participate in, helpful?

In sum, the interview topics for a study analysing the impact of being unemployed and dependent on the unemployment benefit could be the following:

Topic 1: History of unemployment

You would need to know how long the interviewee has been unemployed and why they are unemployed.

Topic 2: Impacts of being unemployed – testing Jahoda et al.'s findings

This theme, following Jahoda et al.'s study, could be subdivided into the following themes: the impact of a) not having a shared experience related to work; b) not having a structured experience of time; c) not being involved in a collective purpose; d) being labelled unemployed and not having any status attached to work; and e) not having regular activity.

Topic 3: Surviving on the unemployment benefit and its impacts

A further theme could be surviving on the unemployment benefit. This theme would examine the impact of the minimal income support on physical and mental health; family relationships; leisure and social connections; and housing affordability and material circumstances.

Topic 4: Budgeting and ability to purchase necessities

This theme would 'measure' the level of deprivation that people dependent on the unemployment benefit suffer. There are robust measures around deprivation so the interview could engage with some of these indicators (Saunders et al., 2008).

Topic 5: Ability to re-enter the workforce

A final theme could investigate the issue of re-entry into the workforce; what is helping unemployment benefit recipients re-enter the workforce and what are the factors hampering them?

QUESTIONS WITHIN TOPICS

The topics should drive the interview and there should not be too many detailed questions within the themes. However, you should note down the questions you want to pursue. This ensures that you cover everything you want to cover. Often, you will not have to ask many of the questions noted as they will be answered in the course of the interviewee answering another question. It is important that the questions are clear, easy to understand and not unnecessarily complex or abstract.

Jargon should be avoided. You cannot expect your interviewees to understand academic discourse or to be part of what Wengraf (2001) has called your 'language community'. The questions should be open-ended. Patton (1990: 296) comments, 'The truly open-ended question allows the person being interviewed to select from among that person's full repertoire of possible responses'. 'How do you feel about being unemployed?' is an example of an open-ended question.

You need to make sure that interviewees can answer the questions posed. There is no point asking interviewees questions that they cannot answer. Patton (1990) has a useful list of the kinds of questions that can be asked. You can ask them about their:

- Experiences/behaviours
- Opinions/values
- Feelings
- Factual knowledge
- Sensory experience
- Personal background

Experience/behaviour questions: These questions ask 'about what a person does or has done' (Patton, 1990: 290). If you are interviewing a person who is unemployed and who has had to move because they could no longer afford the rent/mortgage, an 'experience/behaviour' question might be: 'What did you do when you realised that you could no longer afford to stay in your home?' Another experience/behaviour question may be, 'How do you spend your day?'

Opinion/value questions: These questions involve asking interviewees what their opinion is of something related to the topic under discussion. For example, you could ask an unemployed interviewee, 'What role do you think the government should play, if any, in alleviating unemployment?' or, 'What do you think the unemployment benefit should be?'

Feeling questions: These are questions that aim to understand an interviewee's emotional responses to their experiences. 'In asking feeling questions, the interviewer is looking for adjective responses, for example, 'To what extent do you feel anxious, happy, afraid, intimidated, confident …?' (Patton, 1990: 291). A feeling question could be, 'How did you feel when you were told that you are being retrenched?'

Knowledge questions: These questions ask interviewees about their factual knowledge of a situation, policy or process. These questions elicit what are considered facts by interviewees rather than opinions or feelings. You could ask an interviewee, 'What systems does the job-finding network have in place to assist you in your pursuit of employment?'

Sensory questions: These are questions that focus on what the interviewee has 'seen, heard, touched, tasted and smelled … Sensory questions attempt to have interviewees describe the stimuli to which they are subject' (Patton, 1990: 292). You could ask an unemployed interviewee, 'What do you see when you walk into the job network office?'

Background questions: These questions probe the personal characteristics of the interviewee – age, education, occupation, marital status, etc.

A useful question in many instances is what has been called a 'grand tour question' (Spradley, 1979). These questions ask the interviewee to talk about something they know well and are grand in scale. In an interview with an unemployed person a grand tour question may be, 'Could you tell me how you spend a typical day?'

    If we take the various themes on exploring the impact of unemployment we could compile the following questions under each topic as shown in Figure 3.1. It is good to have the main topics on one page and then you can go into detail. It is important to remember that the interview guide is merely a guide and should be viewed as a flexible 'help'. Ultimately, the questions asked in the interview will, to a large extent, be dictated by the responses of the interviewee. This is elaborated on in Chapter 6.

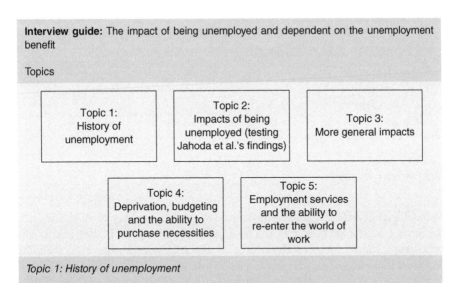

Interview guide: The impact of being unemployed and dependent on the unemployment benefit

Topics

Topic 1:
History of unemployment

Topic 2:
Impacts of being unemployed (testing Jahoda et al.'s findings)

Topic 3:
More general impacts

Topic 4:
Deprivation, budgeting and the ability to purchase necessities

Topic 5:
Employment services and the ability to re-enter the world of work

Topic 1: History of unemployment

For how long have you been unemployed? What were the events that led to you becoming unemployed? Is this the first time you've been unemployed?

Topic 2: Impacts of being unemployed (testing Jahoda et al.'s findings)

(Continued)

Figure 3.1 *(Continued)*

Could you tell me what impact being unemployed has had on you? How has it affected you financially? How has it affected you psychologically? How has it affected your overall quality of life? How has your life changed since you stopped working? What do you miss most about work? Do you miss your fellow workers? How do you spend your day? Do you enjoy not having to get up at a set time? Does the lack of a set work routine have an impact? Do you feel that you are treated differently now that you are unemployed? Do you feel that your status has been affected by being unemployed?

Topic 3: Surviving on the unemployment benefit and its impacts

Has being unemployed changed your relationship with your family and, if so, in what ways? Has being unemployed affected your leisure activities and, if so, in what ways? Have you managed to maintain your social network? Has being unemployed had an impact on your friendships and, if so, in what ways? Have you been able to maintain your health?

Topic 4: Budgeting and the ability to purchase necessities

Are there any essential items that you need to purchase but cannot afford? In regards to your housing situation have you been able to maintain your mortgage repayments/pay the rent? Are you able to feed yourself and your family adequately? Are you able to heat and cool your home adequately? Are you able to buy new clothes? Are you able to look after your health? Do you ever have to resort to charity? Can you afford insurance?

Topic 5: Ability to re-enter the workforce

Is finding a job difficult? What are the main barriers preventing you from finding work? Are the employment services that you have been working with useful? What aspects have been most useful? What aspects have not been useful?

Figure 3.1 *Interview guide*

Another interview guide

This interview guide is drawn from my research on housing tenure and older Australians dependent solely or primarily on the government age pension. My main research question is, 'how does the housing tenure situation of older Australians who are primarily or solely dependent on the age pension impact on their life circumstances?' The research was inspired by earlier research on older people and homelessness that indicated that older Australians in the private rental sector were particularly vulnerable to homelessness (Morris et al., 2005). The housing costs of older private renters are far greater than the housing costs of social housing tenants and homeowners, resulting in older private renters struggling to maintain a foothold on their accommodation. This is a comparative study comparing older homeowners, social housing tenants and private renters. I have an interview guide for each group. The topics/themes are similar, but there are some small differences.

For example, I ask older private renters about their relationship with their landlord or real estate agent. The interview guide for older private renters follows.

Interview guide for older private renters

Topics/themes

1. History of becoming a private renter
2. The adequacy of the accommodation
3. The cost of the accommodation and its impact
4. Finances/budgeting
5. Landlord–tenant relationship/maintenance
6. Health
7. The neighbourhood
8. Leisure and social connections
9. Social and family support
10. Housing options and policy
11. The future

Possible questions within topics

1. History of becoming a private renter

Could you tell me how long you have been living in this apartment/house? Where were you staying before? Was it difficult to find this accommodation? Could you tell me about the process of finding accommodation? Have you always rented privately? How long have you been a private renter? Could you tell me why you are renting privately? Did you ever think you would find yourself in this situation? Were you employed until you retired? Were you married? Do you have children? Did you choose to rent when you were working? Do you regret it?

2. The adequacy of the accommodation

Do you feel the accommodation is adequate? Do you have enough space? Has the accommodation been modified at all to satisfy your needs? Is it physically difficult for you to live here?

3. The cost of the accommodation and its impact

How much rent are you paying? Is it a battle to pay the rent? Would your life be very different if you were paying a lower rent? Has the rent gone up since you first moved in? Are you scared that it will go up again? Can you afford another rent increase? What will you do if it goes up again? Is it difficult to find cheaper accommodation?

Does the fact that you're renting make you feel uneasy? Does it keep you awake at night? What would make you move? Do you worry about living here? Is the rental assistance benefit adequate?

4. Finances/budget

Is it hard to live adequately on the income you receive? After paying the rent do you have enough money for food? After paying for rent and food do you have money left for anything else? Do you have enough money for medical/dental expenses? What happens if an appliance breaks down? Can you afford to fix it? Have you had any expenses over the last year that you couldn't find the money for? Is there something you really need that you can't purchase? Do you ever have to resort to charity?

5. The landlord–tenant relationship/maintenance

How is your relationship with the landlord/real estate agent? Is the flat /house well maintained? Do you feel secure in terms of your tenancy?

6. Health

How would you rate your health? Is your health being affected by your situation? Is your financial situation making you anxious?

7. The neighbourhood

Do you like the neighbourhood? How would you feel about moving from this neighbourhood? Do you have a lot of connections in the neighbourhood? Are the facilities/services good? Would you be prepared to move to cheaper housing in a different area? Do you feel there is a sense of community in the area? Did you choose to live in this neighbourhood or did you decide to live here because the rent was cheaper?

8. Leisure and social connections

Are you able to get out much? Do you ever meet friends for coffee? Does your lack of finances affect your ability to socialise? Are you involved in activities? Do you have much social interaction? Do you have contact with your neighbours?

9. Social and family support

Do you have people that can help you if needs be? Family/friends? What support do they offer? Do you have family you can fall back on? What support do they give?

Do have a social network that you can fall back on? Do you have anybody that helps you around the house?

10. Housing options and policy

Do you enjoy living in rented accommodation? Do you think you would be happier if you owned your own home? Would you prefer to stay in social housing? Have you applied? Do you feel that older Australians living in private rented accommodation are getting a fair deal?

11. The future

How do you see the future?

ORDERING THE THEMES AND QUESTIONS

In a similar fashion to a questionnaire it is important to begin the interview with non-threatening questions. There is no point asking a challenging question at the beginning. It could produce awkwardness or distress and it may impact negatively on the rest of the interview (Leech, 2002). Ideally, the beginning of the interview should be used to establish a rapport and the questions in the early stages should be easy to answer and not induce anxiety. As Frey and Oishi (1995: 100) comment, 'A smooth start also sets the tone for the rest of the interview, establishing a "rapport effect" that builds trust and enhances willingness to participate fully in the interview'. Once the interviewee feels comfortable you can move on to more challenging questions. Of course, some interviewees never feel comfortable and you may find yourself asking challenging questions and the interviewee will not open up. In these situations the responses are likely to be restrained and brief.

The interview guide needs to have a logical progression. The introductory questions, besides being non-threatening and easy to answer should also set the context. An ever-present possibility with in-depth interviews is that they go on for too long and fatigue takes hold. When this occurs the interviewee is more likely to give brief and unhelpful answers. It is thus advantageous to ask challenging and important questions midway through the interview. Of course, using semi-structured in-depth interviews means that the interview can go in a range of directions and much depends on how the interviewee responds to the questions posed. You may find that you have to enter difficult terrain early on. If the question is a logical progression from what has gone before this is not necessarily a problem.

Although in-depth, semi-structured interviews are necessarily flexible, there will be times when it is appropriate to take control. You need to gauge when a topic has run its course. When you move to a new topic, it is useful to flag the shift to the interviewee. You can explicitly inform the interviewee that you are now going to switch topics.

WHAT QUESTIONS NOT TO ASK

Barone and Switzer (1995: 83) provide a useful list of general principles as to what type of questions not to ask in an interview:

The thoughtful interviewer will word questions so as to:

- Probe, not cross-examine
- Inquire, not challenge
- Suggest, not demand
- Uncover, not trap
- Draw out, not pump
- Guide, not dominate

What their guide is suggesting is that the questions posed should not elicit discomfort, embarrassment, stress or hostility. For example, it is not a good idea to ask an interviewee, 'How has being unemployed affected your sex life?' A far less threatening question would be, 'Has being unemployed had an impact on your relationships?' It is important that the questions asked do not make the interviewee defensive. The phrasing of sensitive questions is crucial. Leech (2002: 666) gives a useful example of an interview with a lobbyist about political donations:

> ....[I]nstead of asking a lobbyist, 'Did you give soft money donations?' it might make the question easier to answer to say, 'How much did your organization give in soft money donations?' The latter presumes that it is normal to give soft money donations and that everyone must do it, and also shifts the onus away from the individual and onto the organization.

You should avoid questions that will provide information that you can obtain elsewhere. It could annoy the interviewee. This is especially important when interviewing elites (see Chapter 7) who often have limited time at their disposal.

The questions you ask can have an impact on the interviewee and it is your responsibility to ensure that the power you have as the framer of the questions is used wisely. There is no point asking questions that have the potential to generate a difficult atmosphere.

SUMMARY

This chapter focuses on a crucial part of the research process – developing the interview guide. Prior to constructing the guide it is essential to do some preliminary reading in the area so as to obtain a sense of what research has been done and what are the issues. The drafting of preliminary research questions lays the foundation for your interview guide and should capture what you are trying to answer. You can have more than one research question and you should view the research question/s as fluid, to be sharpened and added to as your research progresses. The construction of the interview guide should be organised by topic or themes. You can then have questions under each of the topics. The topics you focus on should allow you to answer your research questions. Ideally, the interview guide needs to start off with non-threatening, gentle questions before moving on to more challenging topics. The chapter reviews the different types of interview questions and also discusses the questions you should not ask.

Exercise

Construction of an interview guide

- Give your project a title
- Set out your research question/s
- Write out your topics for the interview guide
- Write out the specific questions under each topic

REFERENCES

Aleksynska, M. and Schindler, M. (2011) Labor Market Regulations in Low-, Middle- and High-Income Countries: A New Panel Database. IMF Working Paper. Washington: IMF.

Barone, J.T. and Switzer, J.Y. (1995) *Interviewing: Art and Skill.* Boston: Allyn and Bacon.

Bauman, Z. (1998) *Work, Consumerism and the New Poor.* Buckingham: Open University Press.

Davidson, P. (2011) 'Did 'work first' work? The role of employment assistance programs in reducing long-term unemployment in Australia (1990–2008), *Australian Bulletin of Labour*, 37 (1): 51–96.

Farrugia, D. (2010) 'The symbolic burden of homelessness: towards a theory of youth homelessness as embodied subjectivity', *Journal of Sociology*, 47 (1): 71–87.

Flick, U. (2004) 'Design and process in qualitative research', in U. Flick, E. von Kardorff and I. Steinke (eds), *A Companion to Qualitative Research*. London: SAGE Publications. pp. 146–52.

Frey, J.H. and Oishi, S.M. (1995) *How to Conduct Interviews by Telephone and in Person*. London: SAGE Publications.

Glaser, B.G. and Strauss, A.L. (1967) *The Discovery of Grounded Theory: Strategies for Qualitative Research*. Chicago: Alpine.

Jahoda, M., Lazersfeld, P.F. and Zeisel, H. (1971) *Marienthal: The Sociology of an Unemployed Community*. Chicago: Aldine-Atherton.

King, N. and Horrocks, C. (2012) *Interviews in Qualitative Research*. London: SAGE Publications.

Leech, B.L. (2002) 'Asking questions: techniques for semi-structured interviews', *Political Science and Politics*, 35 (4): 665–8.

Morris, A. and Wilson, S. (2014) 'Struggling on the Newstart unemployment benefit in Australia: the experience of a neoliberal form of employment in Australia', *The Economic and Labour Relations Review*, 25 (2): 202–21.

Morris, A., Judd, B. and Kavanagh, K. (2005) 'Marginality amidst plenty: pathways into homelessness for older Australians', *Australian Journal of Social Issues*, 40 (2): 241–51.

Muir, K., Fisher, K., Dadich, A. and Abello, D. (2008) 'Challenging the exclusion of people with mental illness: the Mental Health Housing and Accommodation Support Initiative (HASI)', *Australian Journal of Social Issues*, 43 (2): 271–90.

Mythen, G. (2012) 'Identities in the third space? Solidity, elasticity and resilience amongst young British Pakistani Muslims', *British Journal of Sociology*, 63 (3): 393–411.

Patton, M.Q. (1990) *Qualitative Evaluation and Research Methods*. Newbury Park, CA: SAGE Publications.

Saunders, P., Naidoo, Y. and Griffiths, M. (2008) 'Towards new indicators of disadvantage: deprivation and social exclusion in Australia', *Australian Journal of Social Issues*, 43 (2): 175–94.

Spradley, J.P. (1979) *The Ethnographic Interview*. New York: Holt, Rinehart and Winston.

Wengraf, T. (2001) *Qualitative Research Interviewing*. London: SAGE Publications.

Wilson, W.J. (1996) *When Work Disappears: The World of the New Urban Poor*. New York: Alfred A. Knopf, Inc.

4

SELECTING, FINDING AND ACCESSING RESEARCH PARTICIPANTS

The selection, finding and accessing of interviewees are essential features of any study involving in-depth interviewing. The 'quality' of the interviewees accessed can make a major contribution to the quality of your study. Locating and accessing potential interviewees can be challenging especially if the group being studied is scattered and marginal. Chapter headings include:

- Who should be interviewed?
- How do I find and recruit interviewees?
- Getting past the gatekeepers
- Do I have to worry about whether my participants are representative of the population?
- How many interviewees are required or when should I stop?

WHO SHOULD BE INTERVIEWED?

The question of who should be interviewed is critical. In all studies there is a particular focus and research question/s and these will determine who you endeavour to recruit to participate in your research. The key premise is that the people chosen should be in a position to provide rich data on the topic and enable you to answer your research question/s. You need to assess which interviewees will be able to provide the necessary data. Although this may appear straightforward, it is not necessarily so. For example, if you are exploring the lives of women who have experienced domestic violence, it is evident that you need to interview women who have been at the receiving end of abuse. They would have a wealth of knowledge about domestic violence. However, even such a seemingly straightforward selection focus could present challenges. It would partially depend on how you define domestic violence. It can take a range of forms and an important question is whether you should only study women who have experienced physical violence or extend the study to include women who have experienced serious emotional abuse. Another consideration is whether you only interview women who have endured extended and constant domestic violence. You would then need to define extended and constant. You also need to decide if you are going to focus only on women in heterosexual relationships or also include women in lesbian relationships. You may want to do a comparative analysis. This could be on the basis of ethnicity, nationality, religion, class, geographical location or sexual orientation. Alternatively, you could decide to focus on a particular grouping. Thus Margaret Abraham (2000) focused on South Asian women in the United States. Drawing on interviews with 29 women she found that a common form of abuse was enforced isolation. After migration the women concerned were cut off from family and social connections. They had little or no independent income, their knowledge of English was often rudimentary and they had minimal knowledge of local law and procedures. In combination, these factors meant that they were highly susceptible to this form of abuse. A participant spoke about how very soon after her arrival in the United States from Pakistan, her husband locked her inside their apartment and would do all the shopping and told her she could not go out as it was not a 'good neighbourhood' (Abraham, 2000: 226).

Shonrah Nash (2005) focused on the experiences of African American women. Drawing on semi-structured interviews with nine women, she concluded that for the African American women interviewed their perception that 'white racism forces African American men to live a socially, politically, and economically precarious existence that is, to some degree, beyond their control' (Nash, 2005: 1431) resulted in the interviewees being defensive of their partners. They were reluctant to report their abuser on the basis that black men were subject to intense discriminatory practices in every societal realm, including the legal system. Fear of their children being rendered severely disadvantaged made some of the victims reluctant to leave their partners.

Recruitment for both of these studies was fundamentally shaped by a decision to focus on a particular grouping that the researcher was linked to by their own histories. It is likely that Abraham would have found it difficult to recruit and interview the participants in Nash's study and vice versa. A researcher's personal history can influence what they choose to research, their capacity to recruit participants and their ability to conduct effective interviews.

HOW DO I FIND AND RECRUIT INTERVIEWEES?

There is a great deal of variation in the accessing of interviewees. The strategies adopted and level of difficulty will depend on your study and who you are targeting. In many studies the potential research participants are visible and not difficult to access. This is especially so if they are part of an organisation or institution and are accessible in a particular space. For example, if your study is about the aspirations and experiences of first year university students, recruitment should not be a problem. You can visit a university and speak to students and distribute flyers advertising your research. You can also advertise on appropriate websites. The university administration may even be prepared to send an electronic notice to all first year students on your behalf. In sum, finding and recruiting first year students for interviews is unlikely to present a major challenge. However, even this project could present unexpected problems. A key issue could be whether the participants come close to reflecting the profile of first year students. There may be ethnic or racial issues. If you are doing your research on Australian first year university students, recruiting Indigenous students may be more difficult. Their history of discrimination and interactions with authority could make them hesitant to volunteer and they may be reluctant to be interviewed by a non-Indigenous person. For similar reasons, African American students may be reluctant to be interviewed by a Caucasian researcher in the United States. In both countries, international students may be reluctant to participate in the study. They may be hesitant about being interviewed in English and anxious about relaying personal information that they feel could compromise their visa status. Another issue that may emerge is that some faculties may be far better represented than others. If almost all of your interviewees are from the Faculty of Arts and Social Science then you cannot really claim that your study represents the views of first year students at the university in question. At the outset, in order to make the study manageable, it may be better to limit the study to students in one or perhaps two faculties. If you focus on two faculties there is then scope to compare the aspirations and experiences of students from the respective faculties. This has the potential to make the study more interesting.

In many instances the recruitment of interviewees is challenging. This is especially so if the potential interviewees are not readily accessible and visible. For example, if you are interested in studying victims of domestic violence, who they are is usually not apparent. Also, they will probably be reluctant to be interviewed by a stranger about what is an extremely painful and personal phenomenon. In this instance you would usually approach organisations working in the area of domestic violence and ask if they would be prepared to assist you in the recruitment process. However, counsellors may be reluctant to ask clients if they would like to be interviewed. If you are coming in cold you would probably need to develop a good rapport with the counsellors so as to build up trust. Perhaps trust and rapport could be established by you doing voluntary work for a relevant organisation. Not only will this allow counsellors to get to know you, but it is likely that clients of the centre will see that you are involved in the organisation and they are more likely to be prepared to be interviewed.

In her study Abraham (2000) discusses the difficulty of accessing interviewees:

> The perception of the problem of marital violence as a private problem, especially in the immigrant community, made access to interviews with abused South Asian women a long, arduous process. (2000: 223)

Her interviewees were accessed over a three-year period. She used three organisations that focused on South Asian women and abuse. Case workers and individuals in these organisations spoke to women about her work and were told that if they were interested they could contact her or have her contact them. When the researcher made contact she spoke at length about her research to potential interviewees. There is no doubt that being of South Asian origin facilitated her ability to access interviewees. A number of the interviews were conducted in Hindi.

Nash (2005) used four recruitment methods to obtain her nine interviewees. Professionals working in organisations that interact with abused women were asked to refer potential interviewees. Some women responded to flyers prepared by the researcher; others were referred by women who had had prior experience with the study and a couple of the interviewees learnt of the study from friends or family. The researcher is African American and focused on African American women. There is no doubt that accessing interviewees who are of a different ethnicity to the researcher, can, in certain instances, be difficult. Making contacts and winning trust can be challenging, especially if the research is on a sensitive topic.

In studies that require interviewing members of groups that historically have been severely marginalised, recruitment can be a lengthy and difficult process. A key element is winning the trust of the people you want to interview. For example, if you want to do research on the experience of homelessness, gaining the trust of potential interviewees can be painstakingly slow. People in this situation would often have a range of problems and may be resistant to telling their story to a stranger. If you were introduced to them by a person they respected, that may be enough. More likely you would have to demonstrate some commitment and perhaps volunteer to work in a shelter for homeless people. Miller and Keys (2001), in their study of the role of dignity in the lives of homeless people, overcame these problems by the first author attending three meetings of current homeless people and 'alumni' – people who had been homeless but were no longer in this situation – at the 'Inspiration Café', a café where weekly meetings were held. The researcher was able to use the space to introduce herself and explain the project.

MacDougall and Fudge (2001) make the important point that in many instances there will be key contacts or 'champions' who you need to contact. These gatekeepers can play a key role in facilitating access and it is important that you develop a working relationship with them and that they endorse your research.

In my own work on the impact of housing tenure on the lives of older people who are dependent primarily or solely on the age pension for their income, the recruitment of older public housing tenants was reasonably straightforward, as many lived in large concentrations in apartment blocks. Once I had made an initial contact with somebody of influence in the building, recruitment was reasonably easy. The recruitment of older homeowners was also fairly straightforward due to this grouping constituting the majority of older households in Australia. However, older private renters presented a major challenge as they constitute less than five per cent of older households and are widely dispersed. There was no space where they gathered. I used organisations that worked with older private renters to publicise the research, but progress was slow. Over a period of three years I was able to recruit about 25 older private renters.

On the other side of the continuum people in elite positions may also be difficult to recruit. They are often time-poor and their elite position may make them reluctant to participate. This is especially so if you are not 'well connected'. However, this is not necessarily true. Zuckerman (1972) tells of how rapidly Nobel Prize winners responded to her request for an in-depth interview. Of the 55 Nobel Laureates living in the United States in 1963, she was able to interview 41 and most replied to her letter requesting an interview within a few days. The recruitment of 'elites', people in powerful positions, requires a formal approach. It is probably best to write a letter where you set out who you are, explain the study and say why you would like to interview the person concerned and how the interview will be used. Richards (1996: 202) suggests that you should '[f]latter] the prospective interviewee by emphasising that his or her input would be beneficial to your research'.

MacDougall and Fudge (2001) have developed a useful series of steps for finding interviewees. An adaptation of their steps is reproduced in Table 4.1 below.

Table 4.1 *Finding interviewees*

Task	Task requirements
1. Establish who you want to interview.	Need to have a clear idea of your research question/s. Decide on the characteristics and geographical location of interviewees.
2. Determine information sources.	Research the organisations, groups and people working with the groupings you want to interview.

(Continued)

Table 4.1   (Continued)

Task	Task requirements
3. Find related research to ascertain how researchers in the area have gone about finding interviewees.	This requires a literature review of relevant studies in the area.
4. Contact relevant organisations, groups and individuals who can facilitate access.	You need to be fully prepared in regards to research questions, aims of the research and interview guide prior to making contact.

Snowball method of recruitment

In varying degrees all of the studies mentioned above have used the snowball method to recruit participants. The snowball method requires that you ask interviewees if they know anybody else who may be interested. This can be a powerful method of recruitment especially when the group being studied is tight-knit and specialised. In one of the most unusual and effective examples of this recruiting method, Wright and Decker (1997) used an ex-armed robber and a small-time crook to recruit 86 practicing armed robbers in St Louis, Missouri. The recruiters used 'a chain of street referrals'. Their own credentials allowed them to build trust and persuade the armed robbers to take part in the study. The result was a pioneering and unique study of the everyday lives, culture, decisions and methods of armed robbers. In almost all studies there would be no need to resort to such drastic measures. It is likely that your first few participants will know people in similar situations. The danger of an over-reliance on snowball sampling is that most of your interviewees could share similar views and you may fail to recruit a diverse sample.

Recruiting interviewees through a survey questionnaire

The use of a survey to recruit interviewees is a common strategy when doing studies that involve mixed methods. At the end of a questionnaire there may be a question that asks respondents whether they would be prepared to participate in an in-depth interview and, if so, to contact the researcher/s. This recruitment method can be extremely effective, but is certainly not foolproof. In a study Wilson and I did that looked at the world of the unemployed (Morris and Wilson, 2014), we initially attempted to recruit participants for in-depth interviews through the use of a questionnaire survey. The organisation we were working with mailed about 200 surveys to their clients who were asked to fill out the questionnaire and drop it back in a sealed box in the office. The mail-out was a dismal failure; less than ten people returned the questionnaire. The organisation we were working with concluded that the poor response rate was probably due to respondents not trusting the survey and sensing that it may be a government attempt to obtain information that could be used to cut off their benefits. Our inability to explain the purpose of the questionnaire face-to-face meant that there was no way of building rapport and trust. Also, with some respondents, there may have been a literacy problem.

Recruitment using the internet

In advanced economies and increasingly in many developing economies, most households have access to the internet. The internet is potentially a powerful tool for recruiting research participants (Hamilton and Bowers, 2006). It is particularly powerful when your research is targeting a group that has a site or sites dedicated to their particular situation. Thus, if you are investigating how family members of people with an eating disorder cope, you could place an advert on one of the websites that supports this grouping. It is important that you do some research and choose the most appropriate sites so as to optimise the possibility of recruiting participants.

The internet can be a critical recruitment vehicle if you are exploring a group that has small numbers and is difficult to access (Hamilton and Bowers, 2006). For example, people with a rare illness will usually have a website that provides support. You could place an advertisement for interviewees on the site's noticeboard.

Although potentially powerful, this recruitment method is not always successful. This lack of success is more probable when the group targeted is highly vulnerable. Members are likely to be suspicious of an outsider wanting to do research on them. Also, even in wealthy countries a proportion of the population does not have access to the internet and non-users will be excluded.

Recruitment through advertising on noticeboards, other public places and media

For some studies this can be an effective and appropriate method. For example, if you are trying to recruit ex-soldiers who have experienced combat there will be clubs that cater for ex-soldiers and you could get permission to place notices on the appropriate noticeboard or to distribute flyers. The notice needs to clearly state what the research is about, who you are wanting to recruit and what the expectations are. Advertising may also involve placing an advertisement in a community newspaper. If you recruit using public noticeboards and advertisements you have to be mindful that the people who respond will be totally unknown to you. If you are to meet them face-to-face you need to consider your security.

Paying participants to encourage recruitment

Paying interviewees has become a common practice. There is no doubt that in many instances the recruitment of research participants is easier when there is a monetary incentive. There is also a powerful argument that participants should be paid for their time (Goodman et al., 2004). However, Head (2009) contends that paying interviewees does have ethical and research implications, and that these are rarely reflected on. She describes her own shift towards paying interviewees. Her endeavour to recruit single mothers using flyers and posters at child-care centres for a study that examined caring and work of single mothers with dependent children was not successful. Over a period of three months she had only recruited three participants. Eventually, she relented and in her flyer mentioned that participants would receive a payment of ten pounds. There was an immediate increase in interest and ultimately she interviewed 20 women for the study. The offer of a cash payment resulted in gatekeepers (family service workers) being far more open to her having access to groups of single mothers where she could explain her research.

An argument against payment is that it undermines the notion of voluntary consent in that low-income participants may feel that the monetary reward compels them to participate (Goodman et al., 2004). This is a contentious argument. Clearly there are instances where an incentive to participate can make a vital contribution to obtaining a viable number of interviewees. However as Head (2009) argues, the payment should be reasonable so as to prevent a situation where people feel they are being coerced to participate. She also makes the interesting point that the payment should be given at the beginning so that participants feel that the payment is for participation and not for what they say.

Another argument against paying interviewees is that payment has the potential to create a climate in which interviewees feel they have to tell the interviewer what they want to know, rather than speak freely. This should not be difficult to resolve and it is up to the researcher to ensure that participants do not have this perception.

GETTING PAST THE GATEKEEPERS

In many instances accessing participants involves going through gatekeepers. This is not necessarily an issue. It can be useful as they can guide you and help you find the most appropriate people to interview. However, reliance on gatekeepers can be a difficult, frustrating and time-consuming process, especially when the gatekeepers have a good deal of power and the potential participants are vulnerable or under their care. A good example of the power of gatekeepers is the study by Kendall et al. (2007) of 'end of life issues and identity' with cancer patients in palliative care. Although they eventually managed to interview seven cancer sufferers and four carers, it was a challenging process. Besides being blocked by some health professionals, the ethics and research committees involved introduced additional barriers:

> … the paternalism of ethics committees … added to the access barriers imposed by clinicians acting as gatekeepers for perceived 'vulnerable' patients, rather than seeing them as individuals capable of making their own decisions. (Kendall et al., 2007: 3)

In any institutional setting (schools, prisons, hospitals, aged care facilities, corporations, clubs, religious orders, etc.) it is inevitable that you will encounter individuals and/or committees who have the power to facilitate or restrict your access. In these situations it is crucial that you first establish who are the key gatekeepers. This can be a complex process in a large organisation and there may be more than one gatekeeper. Once you have established who is the appropriate person or committee, you need to develop a working relationship with the individuals or committee concerned. They need to be convinced that your research is worthwhile and that facilitating access will be in everybody's interest. Usually a formal letter outlining your research and methodology is required. The gatekeepers will probably want to know whether the study will be disruptive and what will happen with the data. If you have received ethics clearance it will be appropriate to make this known and to enclose in the letter the information sheet to be given to research participants along with the consent form. You need to stress that interviews will be deidentified and remain confidential. If you want to identify the organisation you will need to discuss this with the organisation. It may also be appropriate to ask for a face-to-face meeting to discuss your study so that you can address any queries and allay any concerns.

King and Horrocks (2012: 32) make the important point that using gatekeepers to recruit participants does have its dangers, and needs to be thought about and managed. They highlight three risks. It can lead to bias as the gatekeepers (or the people they have chosen to do the recruiting) may only choose participants who have particular views or who they think will give a favourable impression. Secondly, there is the possibility that if participants are chosen by people in authority they may feel constrained in what they can say. Finally, they argue that gatekeepers could force people to participate. This is a serious ethical issue when it comes to informed consent.

The more closed off the institution or the more an institution fits the criteria of a 'total institution' (see Goffman, 1961)[1] the more difficult access is likely to be. For example, obtaining access to prisons and inmates is generally a difficult and bureaucratic process. In Australia it is still possible for researchers to interview prisoners in prison if the corrective services are convinced the research is of value and has the potential to benefit both the prisoners and corrective services. However, access is not always granted. Walsh (2006) endeavoured to interview prisoners and corrective staff in Queensland (a state in Australia) for a study investigating prison release practices. She was denied access to the prisoners under section 100 of the *Corrective Services Act 2000* (QLD). In terms of the Act,

> it is an offence to interview a prisoner without the chief executive's permission, and the Department of Corrective Services' *Code of Ethics* which states that any public comment in relation to the Department or their work can only be made after an 'authorised person has given official permission'. (Walsh, 2006: 143)

In the United States many researchers have abandoned the possibility of interviewing inmates face-to-face and in some instances have resorted to research by mail (Boswell et al., 2005). Access becomes a lot more difficult or even impossible when the organisation concerned does not want information on its workings to be in the public domain. For example, in Australia it is virtually impossible to obtain official permission to interview people seeking refugee status who are detained in detention centres.

DO I HAVE TO WORRY ABOUT WHETHER MY PARTICIPANTS ARE REPRESENTATIVE OF THE POPULATION?

In quantitative research there is a strong expectation that the researcher draws a random sample so that the data obtained can be generalised to the population. For a survey to be viewed as random, each person or household in the sampling frame should have an equal chance of being selected. In the case of in-depth interviews, in most instances, there is no expectation that the sample be random and usually it is not possible. There are qualitative studies where sampling is not an issue. This occurs in small-scale studies where all the potential interviewees can be included. For example, if you are investigating the views of priests on

---

[1]Goffman (1961: xiii) defines a total institution as 'a place of residence and work where a large number of like-situated individuals, cut off from the wider society for an appreciable period of time, together lead an enclosed, formally administered round of life.'

marriage equality it is likely that you will be able to interview all the priests in the geographical area selected. However, in most studies based on in-depth interviews, it is not possible or desirable to strive for a representative sample. The key aim should be to interview a range of interviewees who will be able to give you insights into the research question/s under review. Marshall (1996) dismisses the notion that qualitative researchers should strive to obtain representative samples:

> Qualitative researchers recognize that some informants are 'richer' than others and that these people are more likely to provide insight and understanding for the researcher. Choosing someone at random to answer a qualitative question would be analogous to randomly asking a passer-by how to repair a broken down car, rather than asking a garage mechanic – the former might have a good stab, but asking the latter is likely to be more productive. (Marshall, 1996: 523)

Most studies that use in-depth interviews use purposeful sampling. This involves the researcher seeking out participants most likely to give rich, informative interviews about the research question/s under review. It is useful and expected that you interview a broad range of participants. For example, if you are investigating the phenomenon of long-term private renting, you would want to interview long-term renters who are in the private rental sector by choice and also involuntary private renters – they are private renters because they are unable to access social housing and cannot afford to purchase a home. The comparative aspect adds to the interest of the study.

In his highly acclaimed study, *After Success,* based on in-depth interviews with 20 highly successful people, Ray Pahl, the late distinguished British sociologist, bluntly and ironically recounts his recruitment and sampling method. In the process he astutely sums up purposeful sampling:

> ... I went for chums of chums of people I met at parties ... Sociologists typically do not use the phrase 'chums of chums' but draw up their less than random procedures with pretentious talk of the network and snowball technique or similar ... My chosen method was to adopt a form of purposive sampling. Unlike those ethnographers who spend much time with respondents who are unbelievably tedious and confusing, I tried to find productive and cost-effective respondents and, by and large, the purposive sampling method was very successful. (Pahl, 1995: 14–15)

Pahl's study masterfully examines the question of what motivates successful people (mainly men) to work so hard and the anxieties that drive and trouble highly successful people.

HOW MANY INTERVIEWEES ARE REQUIRED OR WHEN SHOULD I STOP?

This is a difficult question and there is no definitive answer. Glaser and Strauss (1967) developed the concept of 'data saturation'. This refers to situations where additional interviews do not yield any additional data or themes of note. The number of interviews necessary does depend to a large extent on the nature of the study. Some studies are bounded and a small number of participants can answer the research question/s and elicit enough data for a substantial publication and additional interviews will not necessarily yield data that are of note. For example, in their respective studies of domestic violence, Nash and Abraham used few participants. Nash's study was based on only nine in-depth interviews and Abraham, although she had a total of 29 participants, based her study primarily on four in-depth interviews. If they were embarking on comparative work they would have been forced to conduct more interviews. It would appear that in both studies they reached a point where there was a repetition of themes and little new data were emerging – there was 'data saturation'. Guest et al. (2006) drawing on their work with young women in Kenya and Nigeria at high risk of acquiring HIV, argue that if the interviewees are relatively homogeneous as a group then it is likely that saturation will be reached after a limited number of interviews.

> The more similar participants in a sample are in their experiences with respect to the research domain, the sooner we would expect to reach saturation. In our study, the participants were homogeneous in the sense that they were female sex workers from West African cities. These similarities appear to have been enough to render a fairly exhaustive data set within twelve interviews. (Guest et al., 2006: 76)

In my own work the number of interviewees in any particular study has varied. For example, a recent study on the impact of living on unemployment benefits drew on 20 interviews (Morris and Wilson, 2014). The interviews appeared to cover all the themes comprehensively. However, my study of inner-city transition in Johannesburg was based on about 150 interviews. For this study there were a number of disparate groupings I had to interview – black residents who had recently moved into the inner city in defiance of apartheid legislation; long-standing white residents; residents from other parts of Africa (xenophobia was a major issue); landlords; shop and club owners and council officials (Morris, 2001).

After conducting a number of interviews, you can usually obtain a sense of whether you have enough data to answer your research question/s. However, the gaps may only become apparent when you start analysing and writing up the interviews and you may have to return to the field.

SUMMARY

This chapter discusses the crucial task of selecting, finding and accessing interviewees. As illustrated these tasks can vary considerably in complexity. On the issue of who should be interviewed, the key concern should be whether or not a potential interviewee is able to communicate information that will allow you to answer your research question/s. Ideally you should have a diverse spread of participants. The finding and recruitment of participants can be straightforward but can also be challenging. Much depends on the topic. In many studies participants are accessible, but, as illustrated, even in apparently clear-cut studies it can be difficult to find and recruit a diverse sample. There are also instances where the topic requires recruiting interviewees who may be difficult to identify and access. An example given is victims of domestic violence. In these instances you would probably have to make contact with appropriate organisations and request their assistance. Besides using organisations, other forms of recruitment discussed are snowball sampling and recruiting participants through a survey questionnaire. The internet is also a useful way to recruit participants particularly if the group being targeted has sites linked to the issue under investigation. In the contemporary period, paying interviewees is becoming common. In some cases it is difficult to recruit interviewees if there is no incentive. A key issue in many qualitative studies is getting past gatekeepers. This can be a major obstacle and you have to assess whether it is possible. The question of how representative your sample should be is discussed. What is argued is that striving to have a representative sample is not appropriate. Rather, the aim should be to obtain a range of views. The final focus is on how many people should be interviewed and data saturation. This is mainly dependent on the nature of the study. Bounded studies where the interviewees are relatively homogeneous will require fewer interviewees. In studies involving comparisons and a number of different groupings, many more interviews will be required. The researcher has to be attuned to when 'data saturation' has been reached.

Exercise

Selecting, finding and recruiting research participants

Discuss how would go about selecting, finding and recruiting research participants for the following three studies. Where appropriate, explain how you will deal with gatekeepers.

Study 1: 'Just surviving: the unemployment experience of low-wage workers'.

Study 2: 'At the end of our tether: the working conditions and experience of medical interns'.

Study 3: 'At the top of the world: what drives highly successful people?'

REFERENCES

Abraham, M. (2000) 'Isolation as a form of marital violence: the South Asian immigrant experience', *Journal of Social Distress and the Homeless*, 9 (3): 221–36.

Boswell, M., Campbell, D., Demby, B., Ferranti, S.M. and Santos, M. (2005) 'Doing prison research: views from inside', *Qualitative Inquiry*, 11 (2): 249–64.

Glaser, B.G. and Strauss, A. (1967) *The Discovery of Grounded Theory: Strategies for Qualitative Research*. Chicago, IL: Aldine.

Goffman, E. (1961) *Asylums*. New York: Anchor Books.

Goodman, L.A., Liang, B., Helms, J.E., Latta, R.E., Sparks, E. and Weintraub, S.R. (2004) 'Training counselling psychologists as social justice agents: feminist and multicultural principles in action', *Counselling Psychologist*, 32 (6): 793–837.

Guest, G., Bunce, A. and Johnson, L. (2006) 'How many interviews are enough? An experiment with data saturation and variability', *Field Methods*, 18 (1): 59–82.

Hamilton, R.J. and Bowers, B.J. (2006) 'Internet recruitment and email interviews in qualitative research', *Qualitative Health Research*, 16 (6): 821–35.

Head, E. (2009) 'The ethics and implications of paying participants in qualitative research', *International Journal of Social Research Methodology*, 12 (4): 335–44.

Kendall, M., Harris, F., Boyd, K., Sheikh, A., Murray, S.A., Brown, D., Kearney, N. and Worth, A. (2007) 'Key challenges and ways forward in researching the "good death": qualitative in-depth interview and focus group study', *British Medical Journal*, 334 (7592): 521–6.

King, N. and Horrocks, C. (2012) *Interviews in Qualitative Research*. London: SAGE.

MacDougall, C. and Fudge, E. (2001) 'Planning and recruiting the sample for focus groups and in-depth interviews', *Qualitative Health Research*, 11 (1): 117–26.

Marshall, M.N. (1996) 'Sampling for qualitative research', *Family Practice*, 13 (6): 522–5.

Miller, A.N. and Keys, C. (2001) 'Understanding dignity in the lives of homeless people', *American Journal of Community Psychology*, 29 (2): 331–54.

Morris, A. (2001) *Bleakness & Light: Inner-City Transition in Hillbrow, Johannesburg*. Johannesburg: University of the Witwatersrand Press.

Morris, A. and Wilson, S. (2014) 'Struggling on the Newstart unemployment benefit in Australia: The experience of a neoliberal form of employment assistance', *Economic Labour Relations Review*, 25 (2): 202–21.

Nash, S.T. (2005) 'Through black eyes: African American women's construction of their experiences with intimate male partner violence', *Violence Against Women*, 11 (11): 1420–40.

Pahl, R. (1995) *After Success: Fin-de-Siele Anxiety and Identity*. Cambridge: Polity Press.

Richards, D. (1996) 'Elite interviewing: approaches and pitfalls', *Politics*, 16 (3): 199–204.

Walsh, T. (2006) 'The Corrective Services Act (2006): An erosion of prisoners' human rights', *Bond Law Review*, 18 (2): 143–64.

Wright, R.T. and Decker, S.H. (1997) *Armed Robbers in Action: Stickups and Street Culture*. Boston: Northeastern University Press.

Zuckerman, H. (1972) 'Interviewing an ultra-elite', *Public Opinion Quarterly*, 36 (2): 159–75.

5

PREPARING FOR THE INTERVIEW

This chapter goes through the practical aspects that contribute to successful interviews prior to the actual conducting of the interview. Chapter headings include:

- The importance of good quality equipment
- Setting up interviews
- Finding an appropriate venue to conduct the interviews
- Punctuality
- Dressing appropriately

The chapter presumes that you have selected your participants, prepared your interview guide and you are about to enter the field.

THE IMPORTANCE OF GOOD QUALITY EQUIPMENT

The audio recording of interviews has become standard practice and it is highly recommended that you record all of your interviews. It is difficult to take notes and concentrate on the interview; using a digital voice recorder allows you to focus on the interview (Rapley, 2007). Also, recording allows you to capture the exact words used. The way an interviewee describes an experience or their perceptions can be powerful and when you write up the interviews you will often want to directly quote the interviewee. If you are doing a discourse analysis it is essential to have the exact wording. The actual language used by an interviewee to describe an experience or perception is often crucial and has the potential to give the reader a strong insight into the interviewee's world.

There are few things more upsetting and unsettling in the research process than conducting an interview and arriving back in the office or home and finding that the interview was not recorded. Unfortunately, it is not an unusual occurrence and has happened to me on a couple of occasions. You can contact the participant and ask whether they are prepared to be interviewed once more, but usually the situation is irreversible and valuable data are lost. This is especially serious if the interviewee is central to the study and/or was difficult to track down. What I would strongly suggest is that you use two recording devices – a digital voice recorder and your smartphone if you have one (this is what I do) or two recorders. You need to make sure that the recording devices are fully charged or if you're using conventional batteries, that the batteries are adequate. This sounds basic but it is not uncommon for researchers to find, as they are about to start the interview, that the recorder does not have enough charge or the batteries are flat; or midway through the interview, that the recorder stops working altogether.

Digital voice recorders have come down in price and are now affordable. The major advantages are that they are small and thus unobtrusive, generally reliable, you do not have to worry about changing the tape (you have probably never heard of a tape) and the batteries are rechargeable. A major advance is that new models have substantial memory, allowing for many hours or even days of interviews. You can also transfer the audio file directly onto your computer and then send the recording to a transcriber anywhere in the world. A good way to share audio files with a professional transcriber if they are too large to email is through a cloud storage platform such as Dropbox. You can then share the link with your transcriber. As email attachments are usually limited to around 10MB, this is often essential. If you are not technologically savvy, digital voice recorders can be challenging and it is crucial that you master the device before venturing into the field.

It is important that you take a notepad to the interview. Most interviewees do not mind the interview being recorded (Hermanns, 2004), however, you will have the odd interviewee who is not keen. In these cases good note-taking is important. If you are forced to rely on taking notes it is important to focus on the interview and not on your note-taking. Jot down the key points and then immediately after the interview return to your notes and try and fill in whatever you can. The longer you wait the more difficult it will be to recapture the interview. Usually, if a person has agreed to be interviewed they are not likely to object to the interview being recorded. It does depend, to an extent, on your initial discussion with the interviewee. What is crucial is that you make it absolutely clear to the interviewee that all interviews will be deidentified when you write up the interviews and that the recording and transcript are confidential and will be safely stored.

A possible issue with recording an interview is that it does have the potential to influence the interview (Warren, 2002). An interviewee could feel intimidated by the thought of being recorded or alternatively the presence of a digital voice recorder could create a context which encourages the interviewee to give answers which they think the interviewer wants to hear (King and Horrocks, 2012: 44). The topic and the profile of the interviewees are potentially key aspects shaping whether a request to record could be an issue. If you are interviewing gang members it is likely that they will be suspicious and not keen on being recorded. Any study that involves examining activities that may be viewed as unacceptable by the mainstream is likely to produce some resistance from interviewees. In these circumstances it becomes even more pressing that you emphasise the confidentiality of the material, explain the deidentification process and give the impression that you can be trusted.

If you are doing telephone interviews it is essential that you use a good quality telephone. A cordless phone is not recommended due to possible battery issues and relatively poor reception.

When using video conferencing software, like Skype, both you and the interviewee need a stable connection. You might want to use video, or just audio (this might be dependent on the quality of your connection to the internet). It is important to find a quiet place to conduct the interview, so that background noise does not interfere with the call; a microphone can help with this as well. Also, each software package comes with extra features and it is important to know how to use these features, and how they might be useful for you. For instance, you might want to mute your microphone while the interviewee talks. This will prevent background noise on your side from interfering with the call. Also, you should investigate whether the software has in-built features that can record the call, and if it does not have these features then it is worth considering purchasing software that will allow you to record the audio and/or video of the call. Alternatively, you can setup a handheld recording device to capture the audio. Possible issues with the software can be prevented by trialling the software beforehand with colleagues and friends from different geographic locations, who will, similar to your participants, be accessing the internet with varied connection speeds and may be coming into the call from a different time zone.

SETTING UP INTERVIEWS

The setting up of interviews is a key part of the research process. Interviewees feel recognised and respected when proper appointments are made and adhered to. Also, your initial contact with a potential participant can be crucial in establishing rapport for the actual interview. When you first contact a potential interviewee you should follow this basic protocol so as to create the basis for a cordial and trusting rapport.

- Introduce yourself and say what institution you are from.
- Tell them how you obtained their contact details.
- Explain what the research is about and why they have been selected as an appropriate person to interview.
- Emphasise that the interview is confidential and in the reporting of the interviews, interviewees will be deidentified.
- Clarify the role of ethics and informed consent.
- If you are offering an inducement to interviewees you should mention what it is.
- Give potential interviewees your contact details in case they need to contact you.

When you explain the purpose of the research you need to do this in a non-threatening fashion and make it clear that you are keen to learn about their situation and views and not judge them (Babbie, 2013: 316). Ideally, the interviewee should be sent the information sheet and consent form a few days prior to the interview. You will thus need their email address or alternatively their postal address so that you can send them the relevant documents.

It is essential for the potential participant to review the information sheet prior to the interview so that they are acquainted with the aims of the study and can give you informed consent. You can go through the information sheet on the phone and then again when you meet face-to-face. If the interview is to be a telephone interview your institution may require that you receive a signed copy of the consent form prior to conducting the interview. This will depend on the protocols in your particular institution. In the case of a face-to-face interview you should ask for the signed consent form prior to starting the interview. You can collect the consent form when you meet.

You may be able to set up an appointment on your initial contact, however, some participants will first want to read the information sheet and think about their possible participation. If the appointment for the interview is set several weeks in advance it is probably a good idea to contact the participant a couple of days beforehand in order to remind them. When you set up the interview you should not impose a time or day but rather ask the participant what is convenient and, if possible, meet on the day and time requested. You should also ask where would be a convenient place to meet. Of course, the venue has to be appropriate.

In some instances potential participants will not have access to a telephone or email and you may have to make the initial contact face-to-face or by mail. If you decide that it is more appropriate to make the initial contact in person and it involves a time-consuming trip you could try and do the interview immediately after introducing yourself and explaining the research purpose.

With some interviewees it is useful to give them the assurance that it is no problem for them to change the time of the interview if need be. For example, if you are interviewing a person who is in poor health there is a reasonable possibility that something may come up that will make it impossible for them to stick to the initial arrangement. When you set up the interview time you should give the participant your contact details so that they can contact you if they need to change the time of the interview. With some older interviewees I have had to change the time of the interview three or four times. This has been mainly due to the interviewee having health issues.

It is important that you give the interviewee an indication of how long the interview will take so that they can plan their day accordingly. It is intensely frustrating when you are in the middle of an interesting interview and the participant says, 'Sorry. I didn't realise the interview would go on for so long. I have a medical appointment and have to go.'

FINDING AN APPROPRIATE VENUE TO CONDUCT THE INTERVIEWS

What Davies (2000: 83) has called 'the contextual factors' can be an important contributing factor in the success or failure of an interview. The choice of venue is rarely given the attention it deserves in the write-up of research based on in-depth interviews. In some studies the interviewer has little or no control over the interview setting. If you are researching the motivations for engaging in crime among current prisoners your interviews will have to be conducted in the prison (Copes and Hochstetler, 2011). A study of terminally ill people will have to take place wherever the person is situated (Barnett, 2001). These studies are potentially challenging, as you will probably have little control over the surroundings. There are three key issues that need to be taken into account when deciding on a venue:

- The venue needs to be quiet
- The interviewee needs to be feel comfortable
- The interviewer needs to feel secure

You need to be flexible and compromising. There are no hard and fast rules and your study does not have to have a blanket approach – you can have different options for different interviewees.

A quiet venue

A key criterion is that the venue is quiet so that the interviewee can hear what you are saying and vice versa and the interview can be transcribed accurately (Rapley, 2007). There have been occasions when I have been forced to conduct interviews in noisy venues. It is distracting, especially when questions and answers have to be repeated. An interview with background noise is difficult to transcribe and usually there will be gaps in the transcription. At times, a noisy venue is unavoidable. An interviewee may not want you to come to their home and you may have to meet in a café where the noise level will be unpredictable. Also, if there are tables close by and you are discussing a sensitive topic, the interviewee may feel uncomfortable and talk very softly making it difficult for you and the transcriber. Even worse, they may decide that they do not want to discuss a particular topic in a public setting and their answers may be truncated and vague.

Even interviews at participant's homes can be unexpectedly noisy. I recall an interview I conducted at somebody's home where the interviewee's dog could not cope with her owner being preoccupied and she barked throughout the entire interview.

The interviewee needs to feel comfortable

The interviewee should be allowed to choose the venue and method of interviewing – face-to-face, telephone, Skype or email. If the interview is face-to-face the participant needs to feel comfortable in the venue chosen. The interviewee should be given the opportunity to choose where they would like to be interviewed. Often they will want to be interviewed in their home. This can be useful, depending on the study, as it will give you a sense of their living conditions and circumstances. Esterberg (2002: 101) talks about interviewing stay-at-home mothers in their homes and how the children often interrupted. Although this made it difficult to have an uninterrupted interaction and made transcription challenging, it gave her 'much more insight into the texture and quality of the women's lives than an interview in a sterile, artificial environment would have.'

The housing conditions of interviewees can sometimes be dismal and they may not want you to come to their home. Again, you will have to sort out an acceptable alternative venue and offer to cover travel costs if appropriate.

There are occasions where interviewing a participant in their home can undermine the interview. If the topic is sensitive and there are other members of the household walking in and out or, even worse, sitting in the same room, it is unlikely that the interviewee will be frank. They will probably censor themselves to avoid embarrassment or even potential conflict with other family members. If the topic is sensitive you should endeavour to get an idea of their housing circumstances. If they are living in a crowded situation and there is no possibility of privacy, ideally you should arrange an alternative venue.

Some interviewees may feel uncomfortable being interviewed in a university setting. Davies (2000) gives the example of her research with female ex-offenders. She thought of conducting the interviews in her office but decided against it as she felt that the interviewees will probably not feel comfortable in an academic environment and also their privacy may be compromised. She considered her own home but felt wary about revealing her home address and circumstances to ex-offenders. Ultimately she used a range of venues. One woman was interviewed at home; the remaining interviews were conducted in the prison, parole premises or in a café.

The interviewer needs to feel secure

It is crucial that you feel comfortable and secure in the venue chosen. This can be an issue in some situations. If you do not know the interviewee and the contact has not been made through an intermediary, you need to gauge whether it is wise to meet in their home. If you decide to conduct the interview at an interviewee's home, it is important to inform a reliable friend or colleague as to where the interview is taking place and what time you expect to finish. Once you have completed the interview you should make contact with your friend/colleague. If you have not phoned by a set time, your contact person should have a set of instructions as to what needs to be done. Usually you can obtain a sense of whether there is any potential threat when you initially make contact. To a large extent it depends on the interviewee's personal history. Besides the issue of personal safety, if you feel uncomfortable and on edge during the interview, invariably you will rush through it and not be focused. You will want to be out of 'their space' as soon as possible.

The issue of safety for interviewers is paramount and in all cases every precaution should be taken to minimise risk. Some time ago I was the Chief Investigator for an evaluation of an outstanding policy initiative called the Housing and Accommodation Support Initiative (HASI) for people with mental illness. The HASI project involved placing people with serious psychiatric disabilities in social housing. The HASI clients were given the means to purchase all they required to run a home and were also given extensive access to a support worker. The evaluation involved interviewing all 100 clients of the service (a few HASI clients refused to be interviewed). Prior to setting up the interview, the interviewer contacted the support worker responsible for the client concerned. The support worker would give a profile of the interviewee and an indication of whether it was safe for the interviewer to interview the client in their home. In most cases this was not an issue. For all of the interviews we had the time of the appointment and the address. The interviewer was instructed to phone in when the interview was complete. The support worker was also given the details and was asked to be in the vicinity. In some cases the support worker felt that they should be in earshot in case the HASI client became agitated. For safety reasons a couple of interviews were conducted in a public space. On one occasion a support worker's assessment of her client was incorrect. She concluded that a particular client could be interviewed in his home.

During the course of the interview, the interviewee, who was a strong man, became more and more menacing. Eventually, the interviewer made a dash for the door and managed to escape from what she perceived to be a dangerous situation.

PUNCTUALITY

Sticking to the time set contributes to the interview being a success. It is not professional to arrive late and start off the interaction by apologising profusely. In the case of face-to-face interviews it is important that you allow ample time for travel if you are meeting the person in their home or another venue. If you arrive late this may result in the interviewee being 'put out' and their annoyance could have an impact on the quality of the interview. In my own experience, I have, on several occasions, been extremely annoyed with myself for not allowing more travel time. There have been several occasions when the traffic has been unexpectedly heavy, or there has been no parking or I have struggled to find the interviewee's house or apartment, despite using a satellite navigation system such as a GPS or SatNav. Running late also puts you off your stride – arriving at an interview late, agitated and, in summer, sweaty, is not conducive to a good interview. If you are reliant on public transport it is especially important that you allow for contingencies that may delay your trip. If you are interviewing a person who has an exceptionally busy schedule and has squeezed you in, it is imperative that you arrive on time. In these situations it is probably best to arrive at least ten minutes early, as it is likely that you will have to go through security. This can be time-consuming.

DRESSING APPROPRIATELY

It is important that you convey a good impression. 'Impression management', to use Erving Goffman's seminal phrase, is a crucial part of the interviewing process. 'What you wear, how you style your hair, and how you adorn your body send clear messages about who and what you are' (Esterberg, 2002: 102). There is no doubt that interviewees respond to the interviewer's appearance. If they are critical of your aesthetics, it is more likely that they will be wary and not as open as they might have been. Of course, how you dress depends on who you are interviewing and you need to be sensitive to the situation. If you are interviewing students your dress mode should be relaxed. You do not want to arrive wearing a suit and convey the impression that you live in a totally different social reality. This could make potential interviewees feel uncomfortable (Richards, 1996). If you are interviewing 'average' members of the public – retirees, workers, middle level bureaucrats, etc., you should 'look presentable' in the sense that you do not want your clothes and body aesthetics to be a distraction. It is probably advisable to remove studs and cover up substantial tattoos.

If you are interviewing somebody whose role requires that they dress formally you should follow suit (so to speak). Thus, if you are interviewing a business executive or a senior politician your dress mode should mimic theirs. You should dress formally. When he interviewed elites, Richards (1996: 202) took this mimicry to the extreme: 'As a male interviewing a top civil servant, I wore corduroys, a white shirt, tie and a black blazer, and carried a battered old brief case with me.'

SUMMARY

This chapter sets out what is required in terms of preparation prior to actually conducting the interview. A decent digital voice recorder with which you are well acquainted is fundamental. A number of steps are outlined for the setting up of the interview. How you set up the interview is important as it contributes to the rapport between you and the participant. When choosing a venue the needs of the interviewer and the interviewee need to be taken into account. In the case of the former, they must feel comfortable. For interviewers, feeling that they are safe is paramount. The venue should not be noisy. Punctuality and dressing appropriately are fundamental expectations. If you are late and/or your outfit and general style are not appropriate, it is possible that the interviewee will be wary and the quality of the interview could be affected.

 **Exercise**

Setting up interviews

Set up an interview by role playing with a fellow student or colleague. Get the student/colleague to rank your performance and give you feedback. Prior to the role play give them a copy of the key points listed under 'setting up an interview'. Discuss how would go about setting up interviews for the following studies and what you would need to keep in mind.

Study 1: 'Older people on the margins'.

Study 2: 'How CEOs understand and experience their world'.

REFERENCES

Babbie, E. (2013) *The Practice of Social Research*. Wadsworth: Cengage Learning.

Barnett, M. (2001) 'Interviewing terminally ill people: is it fair to take their time?', *Palliative Medicine*, 15 (2): 157–8.

Copes, A. and Hochstetler (2011) 'Interviewing the incarcerated: pitfalls and promises', in W. Bernasco (ed.), *Offenders on Offending: Learning about Crime from Criminals*. New York: Willan Publishing.

Davies, P. (2000) 'Doing interviews with female offenders', in V. Jupp, P. Davies and P. Francis (eds), *Doing Criminological Research*. London: SAGE. pp. 82–96.

Esterberg, K.G. (2002) *Qualitative Methods in Social Research*. Boston: McGraw-Hill Higher Education.

Hermanns, H. (2004) 'Interviewing as an activity', in U. Flick, E. v. Kardorff and I. Steinke (eds), *A Companion to Qualitative Research*. London: SAGE. pp. 209–13.

King, N. and Horrocks, C. (2012) *Interviews in Qualitative Research*. London: SAGE Publications.

Rapley, T. (2007) 'Interviews', in C. Seale, G. Gobo, J.F. Gubrium and D. Silverman, (eds), *Qualitative Research Practice*. London: SAGE.

Richards, D. (1996) 'Elite interviewing: approaches and pitfalls', *Politics*, 16 (3): 199–204.

Warren, C. (2002) 'Qualitative interviewing', in J. Gubrium and J. Holstein (eds), *Handbook of Qualitative Interviewing*. Thousand Oaks, CA: SAGE. pp. 83–101.

6

CONDUCTING THE INTERVIEW

A common view is that in-depth interviewing does not require much skill and cannot be taught. What I illustrate in this chapter is that conducting a quality in-depth interview requires a good deal of skill and that if you adopt agreed-upon practices the chances of you conducting an adequate interview are enhanced considerably. Chapter headings include:

- Breaking the ice and developing rapport
- Conducting the interview
- Follow up interviews
- Can you bring in your own observations, understandings and experiences?
- Interviewing at a distance – phone, Skype and email interviews

BREAKING THE ICE AND DEVELOPING RAPPORT

The first few minutes of an interview are crucial. The initial impression created can play a fundamental role in shaping the remainder of the interview. If you make a 'good impression' and develop a rapport or what Minichiello et al. (1999: 79) called a 'productive interpersonal climate', it is far more likely that the interviewee will feel comfortable and be prepared to open up and answer the questions posed in a comprehensive and frank fashion (Kvale and Brinkmann, 2009: 128). In order to break the ice you need to create a relaxed atmosphere; it is essential that the interviewee trusts you and feels comfortable and at ease in your company (King and Horrocks, 2012: 48). You should clearly convey that you are there to learn about their experiences, interpretations and perceptions and not to judge.

The issue of trust is partially bound up with the topic under consideration. The more sensitive the topic, the more crucial it is that the interviewee has total trust in the interviewer. If you are interviewing somebody about their perceptions and understandings of their organisation's corporate culture (Taylor and Carroll, 2010) total trust is not likely to be a significant issue. However, if you are interviewing people living with HIV/AIDS, it is imperative that the interviewee has total confidence in the interviewer and is convinced that the information given will be treated respectfully and confidentially (Cutliffe and Zinck, 2011).

In his seminal analysis of human interaction, Erving Goffman (1982: 13) wrote,

> When an individual enters the presence of others, they commonly seek to acquire information about him [sic] or to bring into play information about him already possessed.

He goes on to argue,

> Information about the individual helps to define the situation, enabling others to know in advance what he will expect of them and what they may expect of him. Informed in these ways, the others will know how best to act in order to call forth a desired response from him. (Goffman, 1982: 13)

Although Goffman is talking about everyday social interaction, his insights also apply to the interview situation. In everyday interaction if you do not know an individual you will probably be somewhat reserved when you first meet. This is especially so if the person is a total stranger. If they are connected to a friend, family or a colleague you are likely to be less constrained based on the maxim, 'that a friend of yours is a friend of mine'. Once you get talking to the 'stranger' you will arrive at an initial impression that may shape the remainder of your interaction. You could decide that you do not want to pursue the conversation and cut it short or alternatively prolong it and you may even agree to meet again. Of course, this depends on whether you and the ex 'stranger' have the desire or, in the hard-pressed contemporary world, the time to pursue social engagement.

The possibility of making a decision as to how the interaction does or does not progress and the openness of the interaction, is a key aspect differentiating everyday interaction from the interview situation. In a research interview situation, both parties have agreed to set aside a period of time to explore a particular topic. The interviewee is the repository of knowledge on the topic under investigation and the brief of the interviewer is to extract as much of this knowledge as possible in the time allocated. Usually you will not know anything about the person you are about to interview other than that they fit into the category of interviewees whose insights and knowledge will help answer the research question/s you have set yourself. Also, the interviewee will generally not know anything about you, besides that you are doing a study that requires interviewing people like themselves and you come from a particular institution. The strangeness of the situation makes it imperative that you create a good impression from the outset. Although you may have already created a favourable impression when you set up the appointment, when you finally meet the interviewee face-to-face or alternatively start conducting a telephone or Skype interview, the interviewee will again be assessing you and concluding whether they can trust you with their personal information and views. The recruiting of the interviewee through a mutual acquaintance can help dissipate initial uneasiness.

An interesting development is that it is becoming more common for interviewees to research interviewers prior to being interviewed. In certain instances, and certainly when you are interviewing an elite interviewee, it is useful to do some research on the person you are going to interview. Knowledge of the interviewee can enhance the interview.

Breaking the ice is something that can be worked on. In the case of face-to-face interviews, before beginning the formal interview you should:

- Introduce yourself again and thank the interviewee for agreeing to be interviewed.
- Give the interviewee your business card if you have one. It helps create trust and gives the impression that you are professional, that this is a serious engagement and you respect the interviewee.
- Explain the purpose of your research and the role of the interview within it. You should use the information sheet for this. Even if the interviewee has already read it or you have gone through it with them on the phone or in an email, it's a good idea to go through it briefly again.
- Clarify why the study is important and the reason the interviewee has been selected. This should contribute to them feeling that they are part of something meaningful that could make a contribution. You can say how much you value their knowledge and experience. If the study is going to be used to try and influence policy, it is certainly worth making this explicit.
- Make it clear to the interviewee how the interview will work; that you have certain topics you are interested in; that you will ask questions around these topics; they can interrupt at any point and respond to questions in any way they feel is relevant – there is no right or wrong answer (Esterberg, 2002: 102).
- Ask whether it is acceptable to record the interview and explain the purpose of recording the interview. Tell the interviewee that they can stop the recording at any time.
- Collect the signed consent form (you need to do this prior to starting the formal interview) and again stress that the interview material will remain confidential and be deidentified when the interviews are written up.

- Explain that consent can be revoked at any time and no explanation is required.
- Inform the interviewee that if they would like to see the transcribed interview and make changes, they can.
- Where appropriate, it is useful to indicate to the interviewee that you are on their side.

Before starting the formal interview it is often useful to have a conversation about general subjects – the weather, the news of the day, and perhaps, where appropriate, comment on something in the neighbourhood. If you are conducting the interview in an interviewee's home you could comment on something in the immediate environment. A positive statement like, 'I love your garden' or 'your house is charming', are likely to elicit a warm response from the interviewee. General conversation prior to the formal interview contributes to creating a relaxed atmosphere (Thomas, 2009: 161). A useful tactic is to establish whether you have any common interests. For example, you may have been born in the same town or support the same sports team (Rubin and Rubin, 2012: 178). There is increasing agreement with the argument first voiced by feminist scholars that the notion that qualitative researchers should be restrained and remain 'neutral' in the interview situation is misplaced. Engaging in everyday conversation and expressing some feelings and thoughts helps break down the division between the researcher and the researched. Fontana and Frey (1994) conclude:

> As we treat the other as human beings, we can no longer remain objective, faceless interviewers, but become human beings and must disclose ourselves, learning about ourselves as we try to learn about the other. (1994: 373–4)

Goffman (1982) makes the important point (he was way ahead of his time), that in initial social interactions, body language is extremely important:

> There is one aspect of the others' response that bears special comment here. Knowing that the individual is likely to present himself in a light that is favourable to him, the others may divide what they witness into two parts: a part that is relatively easy for the individual to manipulate at will, being chiefly his verbal assertions, and a part in regard to which he seems to have little concern or control, being chiefly derived from the expressions he gives off. The others may then use what are considered to be the ungovernable aspects of his expressive behaviour as a check upon the validity of what is conveyed by the governable aspects. (1982: 18)

He is arguing that usually it is easier to control verbal language and that our non-verbal language can undermine the good impression we are trying to create. In the case of in-depth interviewing it is fairly straightforward to say all the right things at the outset, but it needs to be reinforced by your body language. You need to appear calm and your countenance needs to be friendly. If it is apparent that you are anxious and/or standoffish, there is a possibility that the interviewee will pick up on this and perhaps feel constrained.

CONDUCTING THE INTERVIEW

The material under this heading is perhaps the most pivotal in this book. Ultimately, *you* play a major role in shaping the interview. The rapport you create, the questions you ask, the way you ask them and the manner in which you respond to answers and probe will, to a large extent, determine the quality of the interview and the content (Holstein and Gubrium, 2003: 4). A key feature of the in-depth interview is that you can never predict what will happen. This can be anxiety provoking but it does mean that you have to be prepared and be able to think on your feet. Interviewees and interviews will vary dramatically. Some interviewees will be reticent and perhaps fearful and insecure and have little to say no matter how skilled the interviewer. For these interviewees developing a rapport is crucial. If you can convince the reluctant interviewee that it is not going to be an intimidating experience but interesting and 'fun', it may tip the balance. Fortunately, 'difficult' interviewees tend to be the exception rather than the rule. Most interviewees want to share their experiences and stories and often are pleased that they have been selected to contribute to the study (Rubin and Rubin, 2012: 78).

The order of questions

As discussed in Chapter 6, when you start the interview you should be gentle. There is no point beginning the interview with a complex, confronting or contentious question. It could be unsettling for the participant, their response will probably be guarded and it may have a negative impact on the remainder of the interview (King and Horrocks, 2012: 55). Questions that are sensitive and potentially damaging to the rapport between you and the interviewer should ideally be left to the middle and end of the interview. Of course, you need to ask yourself whether it is really necessary to ask the question concerned. You should only pursue a topic that may cause stress if it is necessary for the study. If not, leave it alone.

At times it is difficult to avoid confronting questions early on. For example, if I am interviewing an older private renter I usually start the interview by asking how long they have lived in their present accommodation. I may then ask where they were living before and follow up by asking what made them move. This question is potentially fraught as the move may have been due to a difficult landlord or them losing their spouse or a financial disaster or a combination of these factors. In the case of Geraldine (pseudonym) she was forced to leave the house she shared with her daughter and son-in-law and their two children. The interview very quickly moved into a highly sensitive area.

Interviewer:	Maybe we can start, so can you tell me how long you've been a private renter for?
Geraldine:	Well, I've been only for a while, 10 September, last year.
Interviewer:	Right, so where were you before?
Geraldine:	I was living with my daughter in a house. We bought a house together and she kicked me out.
Interviewer:	Goodness. I'm sorry to hear that.
Geraldine:	Well that's life isn't it?
Interviewer:	Right. So how did you find the place that you are in now?

Her response to my question, 'Where were you before?' certainly took me by surprise. I empathised with her situation and decided that I would delay asking her to elaborate on her daughter's actions. About midway through the interview she explained why her daughter wanted her to move out.

Once the interview progresses the order of the questions largely depends on the responses of the interviewee. Every interview will be different and it is impossible to predict how an interview will unfold. You should follow up the answers the interviewee has given. This may mean that there are significant digressions. The order of questions is not predictable and in a semi-structured interview you should not feel that you have to ask questions in any particular order. The key issue is that by the end of the interview you should have covered all of the themes in your interview guide.

Do not interrupt before it is necessary

When I read transcripts of in-depth interviews I have done, I often get annoyed with myself as I note instances where I have clearly interrupted and stopped the flow of the interviewee. When you examine transcripts of in-depth interviews it is evident that premature interruptions are a common occurrence. You need to be patient and let the interviewee finish their point even if they are meandering. Let them take their time. If you cut them off you may miss important information. It can also be interpreted as rude.

An example of a premature interruption

The interviewee is an older private renter. I was discussing how he copes on his income.

Interviewee:	I buy according to price and not according to quality or quantity … I suppose not being able to go and have a coffee or something, so some of the things go in the mouth as a kind of compensation or something to make you feel good. So, again it's,
Interviewer:	It sounds like it's been a pretty rough experience.

Clearly, I should have let him finish his sentence. We will never know what he was about to say.

What questions to ask

The interview guide and the responses of the interviewee will fundamentally shape the questions you ask. You should cover all of the topics in your interview guide. However, you need to be open to all possibilities. Other than starting gently and making sure that by the end of the interview you have covered all your topics, there is no standard approach to a semi-structured in-depth interview. How you conduct the interview and the level of intervention will vary substantially and to some degree is ad hoc (Flick, 2009: 171). Certain interviewees will be forthcoming and have a great deal to say. With these participants it is more a case of reining them in every now and then and steering the conversation so that you cover all the topics. The 'steering' has to be done delicately so as to not cut the interviewee off prematurely.

In the case of reticent and restrained interviewees you will have to work a lot harder and think on your feet as to how to get them to elaborate. An interview constituted by very short answers is rarely of any value when you analyse and write up the interview data. One technique is to ask the interviewee to describe a scenario or situation – the grand tour question. For example, if you are interviewing a homeless person about their situation you could ask them to describe a typical day and night (Boydell et al., 2000). If you are exploring academic writing you can ask a student to describe how they go about writing an essay (Starfield, 2002).

The key thing is that you need to concentrate and be flexible. If you stick to the interview guide too rigidly, it is likely that you will interrupt inappropriately and undermine the quality of the interview. You need to ask questions that generate responses that will contribute to the answering of your research questions. Often you do not have to pose many questions and all that is required is an indication that you are listening and the interviewee will keep going. Interviewees usually cover more than one theme in their answers. For example, if you are interviewing ex-prisoners about life in prison and ask, 'Could you describe a typical day in prison', the question is likely to generate a substantial answer which could potentially underpin the entire interview and cover a range of themes. This is an example of a wise interview question. It is drawing on the interviewee's own experience; there is no ambiguity and the interviewee does not have to do any analysis. They merely have to describe their experiences.

WHAT TO KEEP IN MIND WHEN ASKING QUESTIONS

The language used should be straightforward and clear	• The interviewee should have no problem understanding the question.If a question is too complex,the interviewee may misinterpret the question and/or quiz you on what exactly you mean by the question and this could impact on the quality of the interview.
The question should be answerable	• The interviewee ought to be able to answer the question by drawing on their experiences and knowledge.
Questions should not embarrass the interviewee or make them feel awkward	• However, there may be instances when it may be appropriate to ask a question which could make the interviewee feel uncomfortable. Ideally, an uncomfortable question should be asked towards the end of the interview.
You should not ask too many 'why' questions	• For example questions which ask the interviewee to explain things. This could confuse and upset the interviewee. They may feel you are putting them on the spot (Kvale and Brinkmann, 2009).
Time it right	• If you need to ask sensitive questions, they should not be asked at the beginning of the interview.
Be aware of suggesting answers	• You need to be careful not to ask 'leading questions' – questions that encourage a particular response.
Your question should follow logically from what has gone before	• This requires active listening.

Figure 6.1 *Asking questions – what to keep in mind*

If you think of questions you should have asked but did not or if you need more information or clarity on a particular topic, it is reasonable to phone or email the interviewee and ask if they could clarify a particular point or if they could answer a question you did not ask.

Probing

As the researcher you want to obtain as much information as possible in the short amount of time allocated. Inexperienced interviewers often emerge from an interview with minimal quotable material. This is usually due to them not following up adequately or appropriately to answers given. Also, they may not give the interviewee an indication of what is expected from the interview. Interviewees need to know that you want as much detail as possible. Probing involves endeavouring to get the interviewee to clarify, expand or reflect on an answer given (May, 2011). You can also probe by asking for examples. The interviewee's 'interpretative capabilities must be activated, stimulated and cultivated' (Gubrium and Holstein, 2003: 74). Appropriate probing requires listening attentively. You need to be able to improvise and think of ways of drawing out the interviewee so that they impart useful and rich material.

Table 6.1 provides an example of a missed opportunity due to a failure to probe. It is an extract from an interview with an older private renter. She had been living in a caravan about an hour's drive from Sydney (Australia) but had recently moved back to Sydney and was renting a cottage. In some ways the move had been positive.

Table 6.1 *Example of a failure to adequately probe*

Question/Answer	Type of question
It's been great. It's been very therapeutic for me to be with them [her daughter, son-in-law and grand-daughter] and to be useful. And not to be in a caravan.	
So how long were you in a caravan for? *About four years.*	Basic information-seeking question
So what was that like? *It was awful.*	Probing question
Where was it? *On the South Coast.*	Basic information-seeking question
So was it basically an affordability issue? *Oh, no question. I literally had no money. I had a small amount which I had saved and could afford, like $40,000 for a caravan or some such thing, but of course that wouldn't have got me anywhere you know to buy a house.*	Probing question

Can you see where I failed to probe? I initially probed by asking, 'What was that like [living in a caravan]?' The very brief answer, 'It was awful', should have been followed up. I should have asked, 'In what ways was it awful?' Fortunately, later in the interview the issue of living in a caravan came up and I was able to get an insight into why it was so 'awful'. For the interviewee it was not so much the actual caravan that she found 'awful', but her fellow residents and the ensuing isolation:

Interviewee:	It was just that it was just horrendous for me … I don't smoke or drink or any of that stuff, which sounds boring, but that's my lifestyle. And I found there was quite a lot of drunks and things like that and kids screaming and yelling. For my psyche it was awful … When I went to the caravan park, I thought well it's only an hour away from Sydney, but you're getting into a group of people that are not like-minded, … and that adds to the isolation rather than helps to build sort of a community.

A great advantage of in-depth interviewing is that it gives you the capacity to go back to answers that were limited and ask follow-up questions. This does require a substantial amount of concentration during the interview. If possible, you should note points that you want to return to. Below are examples of appropriate probing producing a rich answer. The interviewee had been a homeowner. However, a business failure meant that she had to sell her home and rely on the private rental sector. At the time of the interview she had recently moved into heavily subsidised social housing after an extended period in the private rental sector.

Interviewee:	Well I think I was lucky because it was a friend's home, well a unit in a friend's home, and I did get it cheaper than most. I got it for $250 [a week] and I think it was probably worth $350. I still had a lot of trouble paying $250 … in my case I had to go out and baby-sit and that was all I could do. My husband had kept me very well for many years and I was too old to really get into the workforce so that was the best thing to do. So I looked after children as many days as I could and of a night and but as I'm now 69 it just got too much for me and I was too tired especially with the children, so I cut it down to a couple of days and just a few hours and I'm coping with that, but other than that I wouldn't be making ends meet at all. I really have to earn that extra money to live …
Interviewer:	So it was very stressful I should imagine. [**Probe**]
Interviewee:	It is stressful to me because I've always been used to a home and that was the worst part. Yeah, that's the worst part. You haven't got a [secure] roof over your head. I feel very differently now because

I'm now in a place that they let me in here without a deposit which was marvellous. I only pay $100 a week and that stress is gone. I feel a different person I really do and I've still got the Housing Commission going to offer me another house but I am so happy here. It's quiet.

Interviewer: It's very nice. [**Facilitating, keeping the interview going**]

Interviewee: And I've really only got myself so although it's cramped you know you manage. Much better than being out there in that private market. I was stressed when the people told me I had to go because they were putting the rent up, I couldn't afford it. Very stressful, didn't know where to turn but luckily through community [housing] I just got on to this and I've been very lucky. I look upon myself as very lucky

Interviewer: So what would you have done if you'd not got into this? [**Probe**]

Interviewee: I would have had to be still waiting for Housing Commission [public housing] and living in a bed-sitter somewhere and would have to get rid of all my possessions which would be the worst part. Even here because I started off in a big home I had a lot and over the years I've just had to get rid of everything which is not nice …

Interviewer: So you feel that that part of your identity was being disposed of so to speak? [**Probe, but question is too complex**]

Interviewee: Yeah. I had to get rid of all the things that I liked. So even the last move to here, I had to get rid of such a lot.

Facilitating the discussion/keeping the interview going

Besides asking questions it is imperative that you display interest and indicate that you are actively listening. You need to make eye contact and give a clear indication that you are interested in what the interviewee is saying. This can be done non-verbally – nodding your head, looking interested, smiling and grimacing perhaps. Body language is very important (May, 2011: 142). Verbally, it requires that you use words like 'right', 'uh huh', 'really' and show enthusiasm. Following up on questions appropriately is a key way to keep the conversation moving along. There are times when the interviewee's answer is so rich that it lays the basis for a number of possible follow up questions. You need to keep all of these in mind. There will also be moments where you can share your knowledge with an interviewee and thereby display interest and understanding. When you transition to another topic you should try and do it as smoothly as possible so as to keep up the conversational flow (Rubin and Rubin, 2012: 124). In the course of a long interview it is easy to lose concentration and miss the significance of an interviewee's response and respond inappropriately. Interviewing is demanding and if you want to be on top of your game it is usually not a good idea to do more than two interviews a day.

Concluding the interview

At the end of the interview you should always ask if there is anything the interviewee would like to add. I usually ask interviewees, 'How do they see the future?' If the interview has been difficult for the interviewee you should not leave until they have recovered their composure and you could mention, if you feel it is appropriate, that counselling is available. The consent form should have the telephone numbers of organisations that offer counselling. If you are paying interviewees for their time remember to hand over the cash payment or voucher. You should ask if it is okay to contact them if there is anything you want to explore further; encourage them to contact you if there is anything they would like to add at a later stage and, of course, thank them for the interview.

The conclusion to Cecil's (pseudonym) interview suggests that the interview went well and he was open to further contact.

Interviewer:	And if I have any questions I can always give you a call.
Cecil:	Yes. Sure. Don't hesitate.
Interviewer:	Thank you very much.
Cecil:	And if I move, I'll let you know.
Interviewer:	Okay, good. Keep in touch. If you think there's something that we left out that you want to chat about, just give me a call. You've got my mobile number and it was very nice to meet you.
Cecil:	Likewise.
Interviewer:	And very good luck for the future.
Cecil:	Thank you and I appreciate what you're doing.
Interviewer:	I think it's important research and thanks Cecil for coming out here [to my office].
Cecil:	I enjoyed it. I actually did a course here some years ago. And found it very good.

FOLLOW UP INTERVIEWS

Follow up interviewing can be useful, especially if you are dealing with a complex and/or sensitive topic. A second interview gives you the opportunity to clarify parts of the first interview that were not clear and encourage the interviewee to expand on answers given that were perhaps a bit too brief (Rubin and Rubin, 2012). Prior to the second interview you should give the transcript from the first interview a close read to see if there are gaps and what needs clarification or elaboration. A second interview is also useful when you want to investigate a before and after situation. For his PhD, Benjamin Hanckel interviewed filmmakers who participated in a project on the making of short films for the LGBTIQ community entitled *Stories of Being Me*. He interviewed the filmmakers prior to the public release of the film and then again a few months later. He was interested in whether the filmmakers altered the way they understood and conceptualised their film after the films were publicly released and the impact the making and distribution of the film had had on their lives. A couple of the filmmakers had used the film as an opportunity to tell their family about their sexual orientation and most of them lived in countries where same sex intimacy was illegal and/or highly stigmatised.

Often an interviewee may not be prepared to be interviewed again. They might not have the desire or the time. I generally try and ensure that the first interview ties up all the loose ends. If I need clarification or want to ask a question I failed to ask in the initial interview, I will phone or email the interviewee.

CAN YOU BRING IN YOUR OWN OBSERVATIONS, UNDERSTANDINGS AND EXPERIENCES?

Historically, it has been argued that the interviewer should remain as neutral as possible. However, interviewers are no longer expected to 'withhold their experiences, ideas and thoughts' (Rapley, 2007: 22). The dominant contemporary view is that the in-depth interview is a conversation where both parties give information about their views and feelings. As Oakley (1981:49) noted, there is 'no intimacy without reciprocity'. Fontana and Frey (2008) use the term 'empathetic interviewing' to refer to the interviewer 'taking a stance' and argue that the notion that the interviewer can or should be neutral is 'largely mythical'.

There is some debate as to the degree to which the interviewer should self-disclose (Atkinson and Silverman, 1997). I do not think it is possible to have a hard and fast rule. Each interview is different and you need to assess each situation. There are times when self-disclosure is appropriate and constructive, but there are also interview situations where it is perhaps not necessary or appropriate to discuss your own thoughts and feelings. You need to approach self-disclosure reflexively. There are interview situations where there is a possibility that too much self-disclosure could alienate the interviewee. For example, if you are interviewing a conservative school principal who is a firm believer in tradition, there is little point expressing the view that schools are oppressive institutions whose primary role is to prepare compliant workers for the labour market. They are likely to take umbrage and not be terribly forthcoming for the remainder of the interviewer. If you are interviewing a trade unionist it would be useful to indicate that you are supportive of trade unions, and if you are a trade union member, mentioning this may help build trust and rapport.

INTERVIEWING AT A DISTANCE – PHONE, SKYPE AND EMAIL INTERVIEWS

There has been a strong view that in-depth interviews should be face-to-face (FTF). There is no doubt that conducting an interview FTF has a number of advantages. It facilitates the development of rapport and allows you to get a sense of the interviewee. If you interview a person in their home or workplace you can obtain an idea of the person's living or work context. This can be important with certain topics. For example, if are looking at the impact of long-term unemployment, conducting the interview in the interviewee's home can give you an insight into their situation and how they are coping. If you are investigating decision-making by senior executives, interviewing interviewees in their office will give you an idea of how their status is concretised in the organisation by symbolic markers such as the size of the office, décor, etc. A FTF interview also allows you to witness and respond to non-verbal cues. As mentioned, this can be important both in terms of revealing the interviewee's feelings and giving you clues as to how to manage the interview.

Although interviewing FTF is usually preferable, it is now accepted that using other means to conduct interviews can be as powerful and there are instances when FTF interviewing is not possible or necessarily the best approach. An interesting development is that researchers using in-depth interviews now often ask interviewees what mode of interviewing they would prefer. Hanna (2012) tells of how, in his doctoral research on sustainable tourism, he gave all of his interviewees the choice of FTF, phone or Skype interviews. The most common reason for using phone, Skype or email interviews is distance. If you are drawing on interviewees from a large geographical area, cost, time and, increasingly, considerations of the environmental impacts, mean that it is not practical to interview participants who are located a considerable distance from your home or office. In Hanna's (2012: 240) study, the six interviewees outside of his geographical area said that they 'preferred telephone or Skype interviews as they did not want unnecessary travel to impact on the environment'.

Phone interviews

In-depth interviewing via the phone is becoming common. Certainly, in my own research, the number of people I have interviewed on the phone is similar to the number I have interviewed FTF. Like FTF interviews, what is crucial is that the interviewee feels comfortable talking to you. The establishment of the trust required for a quality interview can be more difficult with phone interviews. After making the initial contact, I email or post the interviewee the information sheet and consent form. I wait for the form to be emailed/posted back before arranging a definite time for the interview. The return of the form usually indicates a desire to take part in the research.

Interviewing over the phone has drawbacks but also has advantages. The researcher and the interviewee do not have to expend time or energy travelling to a venue. For the researcher, the time saved can translate into an ability to increase the number of people they are able to interview. In my own research, especially with older people, interviewees are often not enthusiastic about being interviewed at home and often they do not have the physical capacity or desire to travel to my office. An interview in a coffee shop is potentially difficult because of the possibility that it could be noisy. These interviewees feel comfortable and safe having a phone interview. I always tell my phone interviewees that they can take a break at any time. If I had insisted that the interview be FTF it is likely that a number would not have been prepared to be interviewed (see Sturges and Hanrahan, 2004; Tausig and Freeman, 1988).

An interesting argument is that interviewing marginalised people in their home can be interpreted as yet another example of the 'professional gaze' (Holt, 2010: 115). Often poorer households are subject to scrutiny and questioning within the home by social workers and other professionals and they feel judged. The use of the phone avoids yet another professional intrusion. Interviewees whose homes are a bit chaotic can feel a great deal of pressure to 'tidy up' their home in preparation for the interview. In the case of an older, frail person, this can be a major imposition. Also, some interviewees live in poor and overcrowded circumstances; tidying up in these situations can be challenging.

Researcher safety is another advantage of phone interviews. FTF interviews in an interviewee's home, as discussed in Chapter 5, can be risky and anxiety provoking in certain circumstances. A phone interview obviously removes any risk.

Phone interviews facilitate your ability to take notes as the interviewee is talking. This can potentially enhance your capacity to ask appropriate probing questions.

A final benefit of telephone interviews is the flexibility they offer. In my research with older people I often have to change the time of a scheduled interview due to the interviewee having to go to the doctor or to hospital. It is not an unusual occurrence to phone at the time scheduled for the interview, only to find that the interviewee is not available. However, it would be a lot more frustrating if I drove a distance and then found that my interviewee had had to go to the doctor or had been admitted to hospital. Also, the interviewee would feel embarrassed about the inconvenience they caused. Missing a phone interview is not an issue as it is very easy to reschedule.

Although I have not systematically compared the quality of the FTF and phone interviews I have conducted, my impression is that the quality is similar. In one of the few systematic comparisons, Sturges and Hanrahan (2004) conducted 15 FTF and 19 phone interviews with visitors to a county gaol and the correctional officers who monitor the visits. They concluded that there was no difference in the quality of the interviews.

The use of Skype and other online software

The use of Skype for in-depth interviewing has increased dramatically. If you use Skype's camera feature, you have almost all of the advantages of FTF interviews combined with many of the advantages of phone interviewing (Hanna, 2012). It is an intimate medium and you are able to witness the interviewee's non-verbal communication and, to an extent, their immediate surroundings. However, you are not imposing on the personal space of the interviewee. The convenience of Skype is profound; the researcher and the interviewee can both be ensconced in their respective homes or offices. Another benefit is that you can purchase software that allows you to record the interview directly onto your PC or Mac. Skype interviews, at no cost, allow you to do interviews in all parts of the world.

The potential problems with using Skype are mainly around limited access and technical issues. Many potential interviewees will not have access to Skype or alternatively will not know how to download the program. In my work with older people not one interviewee has suggested that we use Skype. If you do use it, you need to be in a quiet space; background noise can mean that you miss vital information when transcribing. A good headset and microphone are recommended. A secure connection on both sides is essential. A poor connection may result in you having to switch off the camera and it may also affect the audio quality.

Besides Skype there are a number of alternative programs that offer similar functionality and features, such as *Google Hangouts, Viber* and *GoToMeeting.* Some of these programs require downloading software, while for others you can use them within your Internet Browser. When considering what program to use it is worth testing which one works best for your needs and fits into your budget. Importantly, you should consider how easy it will be for your interviewees to access and use the software. You do not want to set up unnecessary barriers for people to participate in your interviews.

In-depth interviewing using email

The conducting of in-depth interviews using email has numerous strengths. It is convenient and cheap and does not require much effort from the interviewee.

It allows you to cover whatever geographical space you want and carry out national and international comparisons. For example, Murray and Sixsmith (1998) researched the use of prosthetics by interviewing 21 prosthetic users in Australia, Canada, the United Kingdom, the United States and the Netherlands, using email. Cook (2012) used email to interview 26 women in New Zealand, the United States, Canada and England who had contracted sexually transmitted viruses. It allows you to contact interviewees who may be impossible to interview FTF and are difficult to reach via the phone. Another important advantage of interviewing by email is that it allows you to interview people who may be reserved in an FTF situation or on Skype or the phone, but who have no difficulty communicating their experiences and understandings in an email. Meho (2006) makes the interesting point that email interviewing removes the interviewer–interviewee effect – class, gender, race, disability, dress mode, body aesthetics and accent become inconsequential or their impact is dissipated. A further benefit is that the interviewee can take some time to consider their answers, potentially enhancing the quality of their responses. The limited research done suggests that there is no difference in the quality of responses obtained via email and FTF interviews (Meho, 2006). A major time and cost-saving feature is that you do not have to transcribe the interviews. Also, you can conduct multiple interviews at the same time. A final advantage is that the interviewees can remain anonymous. This is important when the research is on a sensitive topic. The study by Cook (2012) was only possible because of email. The anonymity and distance enabled the women who participated to communicate intimate details about the impact the diagnosis of a viral sexually transmitted infection had had on their lives.

A disadvantage is that once you send out the interview guide there is no guarantee that potential interviewees will respond to the initial set of questions or to any further questions you may have. It is likely that the quality of the responses will vary considerably and in many instances you will need to follow up on responses. In order to optimise the possibility that interviewees will respond, follow up questions should be done in a timely fashion so that the momentum is not lost. However, interviewees may tire of responding to questions posed and ignore your follow-up questions or give sparse answers. Another drawback with the use of email is that the capacity for following up on responses in a spontaneous fashion and reading the non-verbal cues is not possible. The lack of verbal contact means that the questions on your interview guide need to be clear and precise. Ambiguity could result in an interviewee misinterpreting what you are asking. The ability of interviewees to express themselves in writing could also be a major limitation. If your interviewees are well educated this is not an issue, but if they have limited literacy, an interview by email is probably not appropriate. A serious limitation is that people who do not have access to email cannot participate in the study. Depending on the study, this can be a serious limitation.

The process of setting up in-depth interviews by email varies and presents challenges. In your initial email you should tell the recipient who you are and how you obtained their email address. You need to formally request if you can interview them using email and explain how it will work. The basics of the study should be explained and the recipient needs to be informed as to how and why they were selected for the study. This initial email could contain the information sheet, consent form and interview schedule. Alternatively, it could inform the recipient that you intend to send these once they indicate that they are interested in taking part in the study. Research indicates that when the interview questions are embedded in the email and not sent as an attachment there is a greater chance that the recipient will respond (Meho, 2006). Recipients are hesitant to open an attached document from an unknown source. If you are going to send the documents as attachments it is important to send a prior email informing potential interviewees that you are going to send them an email with attachments.

SUMMARY

The chapter illustrates the crucial importance of developing a rapport with the interviewee and indicates how this can be done. It then outlines the making of a good interview. The order of the questions is important. Ideally, the interview should start gently and the first part of the interview should not be confronting. There are times when this is difficult and an apparently non-threatening question can be upsetting for the interviewee. The questions posed are to an extent determined by your interview guide, but a key point is that you respond to the interviewee rather than slavishly follow your interview guide. The interview should be conversational in that your responses follow the responses of the interviewee. However, ultimately you need to work through the topics that you have identified as important. A central aim of an in-depth interview is to obtain as much data as possible. This requires that you probe, that is, ask the interviewee to clarify, give examples or elaborate on an answer. You should endeavour not to interrupt unnecessarily. To keep the interview going it is important that you respond appropriately not only in terms of questions asked but also in terms of your body language. You need to show that you are interested and enthusiastic. When you conclude an interview it is useful to indicate that you may contact the interviewee if you have any further questions. You should ask the interviewee whether they would like to see a copy of the transcript and if so, tell them that they can make whatever changes and additions they feel are necessary. In most interview situations it is appropriate to talk about your own views and experiences. There is a growing consensus that the notion of a neutral interviewer is *passé*.

There is also increasing agreement that the argument that interviewing FTF is the only legitimate mode is no longer accurate. Phone, Skype and interviewing using email are becoming standard and, in some instances, are essential and do not necessarily affect the quality of the interview.

Exercise

Conducting interviews

Select a topic, draw up an interview guide and interview a fellow student. The topic should be linked to student experience. The interviewee should be able to draw on their knowledge to answer the questions set. Transcribe the interview and note: a) where you interrupted inappropriately; b) where you asked unnecessary questions; and c) where you failed to probe.

Repeat the interview with the same student; transcribe the interview and assess whether the interview has improved.

REFERENCES

Atkinson, P. and Silverman, D. (1997) 'Kundera's immortality: the interview society and the invention of the self', *Qualitative Inquiry*, 3 (3): 304–25.

Boydell, K.M., Goering, P. and Morrell-Bellai, T.L. (2000) 'Narratives of identity: re-presentation of self in people who are homeless', *Qualitative Health Research*, 10 (1): 26–38.

Cook, C. (2012) 'Email interviewing: generating data with a vulnerable population', *Journal of Advanced Nursing*, 68 (6): 1330–9.

Cutliffe, J.R. and Zinck, K. (2011) 'Hope maintenance in people living long-term with HIV/AIDS', *Qualitative Research Journal*, 11 (1): 34–50.

Esterberg, K.G. (2002) *Qualitative Methods in Social Research*. Boston: McGraw-Hill.

Flick, U. (2009) *An Introduction to Qualitative Research*. Thousand Oaks: SAGE.

Fontana, A. and Frey, J.H. (1994) 'Interviewing: the art of science', in N.K. Denzin and Y.S. Lincoln (eds), *The Handbook of Qualitative Research*. Thousand Oaks: SAGE.

Fontana, A. and Frey, J.H. (2008) 'The interview: from neutral stance to political involvement', in N.K. Denzin and Y.S. Lincoln (eds), *Collecting and Interpreting Qualitative Materials*. Thousand Oaks: SAGE.

Goffman, E. (1982) *The Presentation of Self in Everyday Life*. Harmondsworth: Penguin Books.

Gubrium, J.F. and Holstein, J.A. (2003) 'Active interviewing', in J.A. Holstein and J.F. Gubrium (eds), *Postmodern Interviewing*. Thousand Oaks, CA: SAGE. pp. 67–80.

Hanna, P. (2012) 'Using internet technologies (such as Skype) as a research medium: a research note', *Qualitative Research*, 12 (2): 239–42.

Holstein, J.A. and Gubrium, J.F. (2003) *Inside Interviewing: New Lenses, New Concerns*. Thousand Oaks, CA: SAGE.

Holt, A. (2010) 'Using the telephone for narrative interviewing: a research note', *Qualitative Research*, 10 (1): 113–21.

King, N. and Horrocks, C. (2012) *Interviews in Qualitative Research*. London: SAGE.

Kvale, S. and Brinkmann, S. (2009) *Learning the Craft of Qualitative Research Interviewing*. London: SAGE.

May, T. (2011) *Social Research: Issues, Methods and Process*. Maidenhead: Open University Press, McGraw-Hill Education.

Meho, L.I. (2006) 'E-mail interviewing in qualitative research: a methodological discussion', *Journal of the American Society for Information Science and Technology*, 57 (10): 1284–95.

Minichiello, V., Aroni, R., Timewell, E. and Alexander, L. (1999) *Indepth Interviewing*. Melbourne: Longman.

Murray, C.D. and Sixsmith, J. (1998) 'Email: a qualitative research medium for interviewing?' *International Journal of Social Research Methodology*, 1 (2): 103–21.'

Oakley, A. (1981) 'Interviewing women: a contradiction in terms', in H. Roberts (ed.), *Doing Feminist Research*. London: Routledge. pp. 30–61.

Rapley, T. (2007) 'Interviews', in C. Seale, G. Gobo, J.F. Gubrium and D. Silverman (eds), *Qualitative Research Practice*. Thousand Oak: SAGE.

Rubin, H.J. and Rubin, I.S. (2012) *Qualitative Interviewing: The Art of Hearing Data*. London: SAGE.

Starfield, S. (2002) '"I'm a second-language English speaker": negotiating writer identity and authority in Sociology One', *Journal of Language, Identity & Education*, 1 (2): 121–40.

Sturges, J.E. and Hanrahan, K.J. (2004) 'Comparing telephone and face-to-face qualitative interviewing; a research note', *Qualitative Research*, 4 (1): 107–18.

Tausig, J.E. and Freeman, E.W. (1988) 'The next best thing to being there: conducting the clinical research interview by telephone', *American Journal of Orthopsychiatry*, 58 (3): 418–27.

Taylor, J.F. and Carroll, J. (2010) 'Corporate culture narratives as the performance of organizational meaning', *Qualitative Research Journal*, 10 (1): 28–39.

Thomas, G. (2009) *How to do your Research Project*. Thousand Oaks: SAGE.

7

DEALING WITH DIFFICULTIES AND THE UNEXPECTED

Interviewing doesn't always go according to plan. In this chapter I discuss what can go wrong in an interview situation and how to deal with difficulties. Possible problems could include the interviewer or the interviewee feeling insecure in the venue, the interviewee refusing to sign the consent form or not being prepared to be audio-taped. A major and not unusual difficulty is the interviewee giving answers that are too brief to use. Ways to address these problems are discussed. Another potential concern is with the interviewer and the interviewee coming from different backgrounds. This concern leads to important questions. What impact does 'difference' have on the interview interaction? If it is an issue, how can it be overcome? Interviewing vulnerable populations presents a particular challenge. Chapter headings include:

- What to do if a potential interviewee is reluctant to sign the consent form or have the interview recorded
- What to do if you feel insecure in an interviewing situation
- The highly sensitive interview
- The uncommunicative interviewee
- Strategies for turning interviews around
- Interviewing across difference
- Interviewing across race
- Interviewing in Indigenous communities
- Sexual orientation of the interviewer
- Interviewing disabled people

- Interviews with second language speakers
- Interviewing elites
- Interviewing people who are disadvantaged and marginalised

WHAT TO DO IF A POTENTIAL INTERVIEWEE IS RELUCTANT TO SIGN THE CONSENT FORM OR HAVE THE INTERVIEW RECORDED

Occasionally, you may arrive for an interview and find the person refuses to sign the consent form. This is obviously a difficult situation. You could say, 'never mind' and walk away, or alternatively endeavour to establish why they are having second thoughts. Probably the most common reason for an interviewee refusing to take part after initially agreeing is the fear that they will be identified and/or misquoted. For the former concern you can try and convince them that the data will be deidentified and they have nothing to worry about. To allay fears of being misquoted you could say that you will send them the transcript to scrutinise and invite them to check for accuracy. Fortunately, refusing to sign the consent form after initially agreeing to being interviewed is a rare occurrence.

A more likely scenario but also unusual, is an interviewee not being keen on the interview being recorded. Again, you need to emphasise that the data are confidential and will be deidentified. Also, you should explain why it is necessary to record the interview, that is, if you are going to quote the interviewee, you need an exact record. You could suggest compromises. One compromise is that you record the interview, transcribe it and then send it to the interviewee who can then note which parts they do not want quoted. Alternatively, during the interview they can ask for a particular section to be off the record. The worst-case scenario is that you agree not to audio-tape and rely on note-taking.

WHAT TO DO IF YOU FEEL INSECURE IN AN INTERVIEWING SITUATION

Finding yourself in a risky situation is something you want to avoid. However, there are topics that lend themselves to researchers finding themselves in dangerous settings (Bloor et al., 2007). Lee (1995) distinguishes between 'ambient danger' and 'situational danger'. The former refers to doing research in dangerous settings, for example research in a conflict zone or on youth gangs. Situational danger refers to the presence of the researcher provoking a dangerous situation. There will be situations where there is both ambient and situational danger. In-depth interviewing as a method does mean that there may be times when you have to conduct interviews in settings that are unfamiliar and unpredictable. I did my work on inner-city transition in Johannesburg during the last years of the apartheid government (Morris, 1999). Many of the apartment blocks in the high density area that was the site of my research, were occupied by aggrieved and poor tenants and at times, when I entered a building to look for the person I wanted to interview (I had their contact details and they were expecting me), I found myself in circumstances which were unpredictable and anxiety provoking. This was mainly in the common areas, especially stairwells and lifts. However, there were occasions when I felt apprehensive in the apartment of interviewee's. Although I did all my interviews during the day, on reflection, it was probably unwise to go to interviewee's homes unaccompanied. At the very least I should have arranged to meet interviewees outside their building so that they could escort me to their apartment.

Over the last two decades institutions have become more concerned about duty of care and researcher's safety – what Howell (1990) termed the 'human hazards of fieldwork'. At present there are whole swathes of social reality that are virtually out of bounds for social research. These are often in 'frontier zones', zones which are virtually unpoliced and where there is a real danger of a social researcher being assaulted or worse. A whole country can become a frontier zone – for example, contemporary Syria or Iraq. Any study of people involved in illicit activity is potentially dangerous; criminal gangs are an obvious example. Despite the tightening up of ethics there are still instances where researchers find themselves in dangerous situations. Belousov et al. (2007) tell of their comparative research on the enforcement of international health and safety regulations by inspectors in the shipping industry. Shortly after they embarked on the research, the key person organising access to the port workers in St Petersburg was gunned down outside his home. Although the researchers were confident that the killing had nothing to do with their research project, it had significant ramifications. Potential informants became reticent and uncooperative and for a period of time all research was suspended as it was felt that it was too dangerous for the fieldworkers to operate.

Sampson and Thomas (2003) describe the ambient and situational dangers they experienced as female researchers studying transnational seafarer communities. They conducted their research at sea and were stuck in totally male-dominated situations for weeks at a time with no escape. Besides the risk of sexual assault there were 'ambient' risks. Accidents at sea are common and the lack of access to medical personnel means that illnesses that are benign if treated timeously can be deadly on board ship.

If you manage to obtain ethics clearance and find yourself doing research that involves situations which are potentially risky, you should do a risk assessment for each interview and reflect on whether you should proceed and if you do proceed, how you can lessen the risk. The easiest way to lessen the risk is to conduct the research in a safe venue. If this is not possible you should consider the following strategies:

- Conduct the interview in pairs if possible
- Alternatively, have someone accompany you to the interview. Female researchers are more vulnerable so having a male companion can be important
- Give a colleague clear details as to where you are going and make sure they have your mobile phone number
- Always carry a mobile phone and make sure it is charged
- Arrange to call a reliable friend/colleague when you have finished the interview
- If you do not call by a certain time, the friend/colleague that you have given your details to should call you
- Instruct them to call the relevant authorities if you cannot be contacted

If you are doing your interviews in another country you should visit your government's website to assess the risk prior to departure and make sure you have adequate funding.

THE HIGHLY SENSITIVE INTERVIEW

As discussed in Chapters 2 and 6, some topics can be highly sensitive and cause distress. Occasionally, the distress may be so intense that the interview has to be cut short. This needs to be done in an empathetic and caring fashion. In most cases the interviewee will recover their composure after a short break, and you will be able to continue the interview. If the interviewee is too upset to continue, a difficult question is whether you should ask the interviewee for another interview. In certain circumstances this may be appropriate. The interviewee may welcome the opportunity to again talk about the issues that provoked the initial distress and might feel more ready to talk about them. On the other hand, if it is evident that the subject matter is deeply upsetting for the interviewee concerned it is probably wise not to pursue the interviewee in question. You should give the interviewee details of a counselling service that they can access.

Sensitive topics should not necessarily be off limits. Some interviewees find participating in a sensitive study beneficial. For example, Stroebe et al. (2003) found that in their studies of bereavement, some people agreed to participate as they wanted to share their experience and they saw it as a way of coming to terms with their loss and perhaps helping others. What is crucial is that interviewees are dealt with sensitively. You need to be thoughtful when probing and ask yourself whether your questions might be too emotional and stressful for the interviewee. As Adamson and Holloway (2012: 739) state, 'In sensitive interviewing there may be a research dilemma in deciding whether to probe or whether to respect apparent reluctance to discuss a particular issue.'

Sensitive topics can also have an impact on the interviewer (Lee and Lee, 2012: 45). A question to ask yourself prior to embarking on a sensitive topic is whether you will cope emotionally. There is increasing awareness of the potential impact on the researcher of engaging in sensitive research. Reflecting on her research on domestic violence, Chatzifotiou (2000) commented,

> For me, the discovery of the amount of pain in women's lives reverberated for some time, particularly when I conducted the very first interviews. During and after each interview I usually felt overwhelmed and became anxious and depressed. (2000: 8.1)

Often there is a failure on the part of the interviewer to recognise that the research they are embarking on could have an emotional impact. If your research is having an impact on your mental health you should take appropriate steps. This may involve talking to a counsellor, stopping the research for a while, debriefing with colleagues or spacing out the interviews so as to dissipate the intensity.

THE UNCOMMUNICATIVE INTERVIEWEE

Although all interviews produce 'partial truths' (Clifford, 1986) and 'unavoidable indeterminancy of meaning' (Miller, 2011) there is an expectation that they produce data that can be utilised in your analysis. However, 'failed' interviews are not unusual. A failed interview can be defined as an interview that is barely or not at all usable due to the answers being too brief, unclear or off the topic. An interview that is constituted mainly by yes and no answers is not much use. Interviewees may be reticent for a range of reasons and if an interview is going 'badly' you need to establish why this is so. It may be due to linguistic and cultural differences; minimal capacity to answer the questions posed due to poor framing of questions; active resistance to the interview convention; or an inability by interviewees to articulate detailed answers due to a lack of trust, fear, language difficulties or simply having nothing to say. Some issues are easier to deal with. If an interviewee is worried about confidentiality you can again explain how the data will be stored and deidentified. In some cases, interviewees who have no idea of the research interview convention may think that giving short answers is the right approach or that they should not give details which may upset you. You need to make sure that interviewees are fully aware of the research interview genre – that frank, detailed answers are expected and that there is no right or wrong answer. Interviews where interviewees are having difficulty understanding the questions; articulating their answers or who are actively resisting the interviewer are extremely difficult if not impossible to rescue.

STRATEGIES FOR TURNING INTERVIEWS AROUND

It has been argued that 'failed' interviews often have much to teach us and that by reflecting on why an interview failed we can strengthen our interviewing abilities (Prior, 2014). There are interviews that cannot be rescued. The forces against the interview being successful are simply too great and beyond your control. What is important is not to take a 'failed interview' personally. Rather, reflect on the issues possibly contributing to 'interview failure' and if possible try and eliminate the stumbling blocks for the next round of interviews. For a start, assess whether the chosen interviewee was suitable. Perhaps they simply did not have the knowledge to engage with the topic. Secondly, take a 'good look' at your interview topics and interview style. You need to ask yourself whether your preparation for the interview was adequate. Perhaps the questions posed were too complex or threatening. Review your style of interviewing. What is useful is to carefully go through your transcripts and assess how your 'interviewer talk' shaped the interview/s. Perhaps the questions posed encouraged 'yes' and 'no' responses rather than discussion; they were too 'closed'. Interviews that are dominated by answers that are very brief or unhelpful may indicate that the questions were too complex and the interviewee did not have a clear sense of what you were asking. Alternatively, the interviewee may have decided that the questions were too threatening and they were not prepared to give details. Another possibility is that the interviewee did not have the linguistic skills required to answer the question.

There are other issues you can think about. Perhaps your own demeanour is working against you obtaining quality data. Are you dressing appropriately and using a suitable venue? Are you establishing the rapport necessary? Perhaps you are launching into the formal interview without spending the time required to gain the trust of the interviewee. This is especially significant if you are dealing with a sensitive topic. Assess whether you are coming across as anxious or not having the necessary knowledge. If you are discernibly anxious, and/or do not have requisite knowledge there is a danger that interviewees may not take you seriously. You could work on your anxiety by perhaps interviewing a friend and asking them to role play.

Key contributors to 'failed interviews' are unnecessary interruptions and inadequate probing. You need to study your transcript/s to see where you interrupted inappropriately and disturbed the flow of the conversation and where you should have probed but did not. The failure to adequately probe is probably the main reason why interviews fail. Skilled probing requires careful listening and responding appropriately. Assess whether you are listening intensely enough and whether your responses are adequate. Ask yourself whether you are letting potentially important points sink without a trace. Like any skill the more interviews you conduct, the more accomplished you will become. However, analysing transcripts of failed interviews (and successful interviews) and reflecting on where you could have or should have done things differently ought to hasten your transition into a skilled interviewer. In-depth interviews are complex interactions and by examining your transcripts you can gain insight into how you are perhaps contributing to your interviews not reaching their potential.

During the actual interview there are strategies you could adopt to perhaps rescue an interview that is eliciting little detail. Getting interviewees to tell a story rather than respond to actual questions can be powerful. For example, if you are examining working conditions and exploitation of workers in precarious situations instead of asking about the precise nature of the exploitation, you could ask the interviewee to describe a typical working day (Bohle et al., 2004).

If it is evident that an interviewee is not really 'getting' your question, do not be concerned about phrasing the question in different ways. Roulston (2011) suggests proposing possible responses for an interviewee can be a useful technique for generating responses. The interviewee can agree or disagree with your suggestion and hopefully elaborate. You could, for example, ask an unemployed young person, '*So you don't work because there are no jobs or because you are lazy?*' The latter suggestion is likely to provoke a vehement denial and hopefully elicit detail on the difficulties of finding employment. This is potentially a risky strategy and you would need to 'read' the interviewee so as to assess what is an appropriate way to elicit more detail.

If your interview is not going well and needs rescuing, here are some questions to ask yourself:

- Are the interviewees you have recruited appropriate?
- Is your interview guide clear?
- Can the interviewees understand your questions?
- Is the venue for the interviews suitable?
- Is your dress mode off-putting?
- Are you developing a rapport with your interviewees?
- Are you too anxious?
- Are you adequately prepared?
- Do you have the requisite knowledge?
- Are you interrupting inappropriately
- Is your probing adequate?

And you could also use the following strategies if your interview is going poorly:

- Ask the interviewee to tell a story rather than pose a direct question
- Pose the same question in different ways
- Suggest possible responses

You need to read through your transcripts carefully to see whether and where you interrupted unnecessarily; did not probe when you should have; and whether the way you posed a question made it difficult for the interviewee to understand what you were asking.

INTERVIEWING ACROSS DIFFERENCE

Another reason for interviews not going according to plan is when you interview across difference. There are instances when this can have a major impact. Feminist research has made researchers far more aware and reflexive of power relationships in research and how knowledge is constructed in the interviewer–interviewee relationship. Ann Oakley's (1981) seminal article on interviewing women illustrated how women responded to her as a feminist researcher and how historically interviewing had been dominated by a 'masculine paradigm' in that the interview was characterised by a hierarchy whereby the interviewee was expected to answer questions posed and the interviewer was to evade any questions asked by the interviewee. In this model of interviewing, disclosure by the interviewer is actively discouraged on the basis that it is inappropriate and could lead to bias. As discussed in Chapter 6, this notion of how interviews should be conducted has been robustly critiqued and the dominant contemporary view is that the interviewer should share their opinions and engage with the interviewee to dissipate the power relations and division between the researcher and the researched.

Feminist researchers contend that gender continues to be pertinent and cross sex interviewing can lead to a limited interview due to the heavily gendered cultural and social context in which we live (Fontana and Frey, 2008: 135). It is argued that a female interviewee is more likely to develop a rapport and open up with a female interviewer. There is little doubt that with some topics this is likely. For example, in the case of Ann Oakley's research, *Becoming a Mother*, it is highly unlikely that interviewees would have been forthcoming about pregnancy, childbirth, intimacy post childbirth, etc. with a male interviewer. However, the interviewer and the interviewee being of the same sex certainly does not guarantee interviewer–interviewee rapport or success. Wasserfall (1993: 23) makes the important point that the notion of commonality among women ignores 'enormous differences' in regards to 'power, culture, belief, political commitments, ethnicity [and] class [that] cannot be easily transcended'. A female researcher may not have much in common with a female interviewee other than their sex.

Each study is unique and with every study you need to reflect on whether it is appropriate for you to be doing the research under consideration. The argument that you should always be of the same class, gender, 'race', nationality, ethnicity and sexual orientation as the interviewee is debatable and it is not necessarily accurate to conclude that physical and social similarity will necessarily lead to a superior or more empathetic interview (Reinharz and Chase, 2001). The crucial issue is that the interviewer needs to be sensitive to difference and power differentials and recognise that they can have an influence. Rubin and Rubin (1995) conclude that there is a tendency to overestimate the difficulties of interviewing across difference,

In fact, interviewing people similar to yourself can pose difficulties, because the interviewees assume that you know what they know. They may not explain taken-for-granted meanings in the way they would to an outsider. (1995: 111)

They refer to a study by Tixier y Vigil and Elsasser (1978) that compared the interviews of Chicana women, carried out by Anglo women, and those of Chicana women carried out by Chicana women. They found that the Chicana women spoke more freely to the Anglo interviewer about 'sex-related matters' and that on the issues of discrimination and prejudice it made no difference as to who the interviewer was. Another example is provided by Dyck (1997). She endeavoured to ensure that the interviewer and interviewee were of the same ethnicity. However, some of the interviewees were reluctant to share information with a person 'of the same community' and preferred to be interviewed by the researcher. In her 2001 article Smith tells of the difficulty her research assistant had interviewing Maori and Pacific Island youth even though he was a Pacific Islander and a 'former street toughie with an attitude'.

An important argument made by Nairn et al. (2005: 236) is that in the case of marginalised groups if the 'other' (a member of a marginalised group) is employed to interview the 'other', then members of the dominant group may never get to interview the other (people who are part of marginalised groups). They would only interview members of their own group. They would also be analysing data they never collected.

There are certainly topics where the interview is likely to yield richer insights if the interviewer and the interviewee come from similar backgrounds. If you want to examine domestic violence against women through the use of in-depth interviews, it will be a difficult task if you are male and arguably not an appropriate topic for a male to pursue. As indicated in Chapter 4, at times not only sex but also nationality or ethnicity can be barriers. Thus if you want to explore domestic violence against Tamil women, your task will almost certainly be made easier if you are Tamil and female. Commonality will help with recruitment, interview guide construction (you will be aware of many of the issues which may be specific to the grouping you are investigating), and the quality of the interview. Tamil women are more likely to trust and open up to a Tamil female interviewer.

INTERVIEWING ACROSS RACE

Unfortunately, racism continues to be a feature of contemporary society and we cannot discount race-of-interviewer effects. Being an 'insider' (of the same race) can be helpful in the interviewing interaction. Reflecting on her qualitative study of African American women re-entering education, Johnson-Bailey (1999: 699) concludes,

> There were silent understandings, culture bound phrases that did not need interpretation, and nonverbalised answers conveyed with culture-specific hand gestures and facial expressions laced throughout the dialogue. (1999: 699)

Being a different skin colour to your interviewee does not preclude the possibility of developing rapport and trust and conducting an effective interview but it can make it more challenging. With some studies across race it may not be enough to organise interviews and appear at the appointed time; you may have to illustrate that you are committed to the cause in question. Marks (2001) did a brilliant study of young militant black activists in Soweto and surrounds at the height of the anti-apartheid struggle. Despite being white, she could access interviewees because she was highly involved in the anti-apartheid struggle and was thus trusted. Young black activists opened up to her (being close in age also helped) and told her the most remarkable stories. She was also able to safely traverse extremely dangerous and unpredictable spaces to access participants.

Rhodes (1994: 548) makes the interesting argument that although the skin colour of an interviewer will impact on the way interviewees respond, 'it is erroneous to assume that a qualitative difference necessarily implies that one type of account is intrinsically superior to another'. Thus the interview conducted by a white interviewer is likely to be different to an interview conducted by a black interviewer, but it does necessarily mean that there will be differences in quality. Also, the impact will depend on the context; if the study is being conducted in a deeply racist milieu it is more likely that black interviewees will be suspicious of a white interviewer and guarded in their responses. The subject matter is also important. Studies that have as their focus issues around race will invariably be more contentious and the race-of-interviewer effect could be significant (Davis, 1997). The effects may work in both directions. For example, in the case of black interviewees, they may give responses that they think the white interviewer will want to hear and if interviewed by a black interviewer they may be more prone to give responses that suggest they are firmly aligned with black causes and they are not 'sell-outs' (Davis, 1997).

The interviewer effect can be subtle. In a study of the role of racism in the Hurricane Katrina tragedy (most of the nearly 2000 who died as a result of Katrina were from poor African American households), 41 African American interviewees were asked, 'Do you think race played a part in what happened with Hurricane Katrina?' Although the skin colour of interviewers was not a factor in determining whether interviewees felt that race played a role, it did impact on the way interviewees stated their position. Interviewees who were interviewed by white interviewers 'were significantly more likely to use qualifying statements, to contradict previous statements, and to assert that members of other racial groups were also victims of the hurricane' (Lowe et al., 2011: 54). Those interviewed by African American interviewers were far less ambiguous about stating that racism was a central feature of the Hurricane Katrina tragedy.

INTERVIEWING IN INDIGENOUS COMMUNITIES

The history of colonialism has made interviewing Indigenous people by non-Indigenous researchers particularly fraught (Fletcher, 2003; Hunter, 2001). Research 'on' Indigenous communities by non-Indigenous researchers is often viewed with suspicion and the inevitable questions are why is the research being conducted, what will it be used for and who will benefit (Kenny, 2004). In order for research in Indigenous communities to be successful, a community-based participatory research (CBPR) approach is usually essential.

> [CBPR] recognises the importance of including local conditions and community experts in designing their research … In this way research designs are no longer based solely on Western science, but incorporate Aboriginal and Indigenous ways of knowing. (Fletcher, 2003: 29)

CBPR requires substantial consultation with the community from the outset. Part of this process will involve working with the community to develop the interview guide. The actual interview can be challenging; direct questions may not work.

Meadows et al. (2003) commented that they had to change their interviewing style – 'Recognizing that women familiar with an oral tradition background were likely to be more comfortable sharing stories than answering direct questions …'. The issues within Indigenous communities are usually so profound that there is a strong expectation that any research conducted should contribute to overcoming the legacies of colonialism and discrimination.

SEXUAL ORIENTATION OF THE INTERVIEWER

In the case of qualitative research on the gay, lesbian, bisexual and transgender (GLBT) community, the sexual orientation of the researcher can certainly be an important factor. It has been argued that if you are an 'insider', your interviews are likely to be stronger. LaSala (2003) comments,

> Insider researchers' personal familiarity with issues affecting their respondents' lives may enable them to formulate research questions and hypotheses that might not occur to outsiders … For example, because I am a gay man, I am conscious of how commonly held ideas about relationships may not fit everyone. (2003: 17–18)

He notes that the sexual orientation of the interviewer could have a major impact on the framing and conducting of the research:

> Divergent insider and outsider perspectives could result in strikingly different studies of the same phenomenon, and lead to markedly different conclusions being drawn from similar data. (2003: 18)

Being an insider also facilitated his ability to recruit interviewees and develop appropriate interview questions. Interviewees felt that they could trust him and be 'honest' due to his familiarity with their experiences.

Interestingly LaSala emphasises that although being an insider does have major advantages it can also be a limitation in that the intense familiarity may result in a GLBT interviewer missing key issues. Another potential limitation is that an insider talking to an insider may fear disclosing negative information especially if the researcher is from the same city. Of course, like any study involving interviewing you need to obtain the trust of the interviewees and this is not necessarily guaranteed just because you are an insider: 'trust must be gained even by GLBT researchers studying populations to which they belong' (Meezan and Martin, 2003: 11).

Benjamin Hanckel, who at the time of writing was doing doctoral research on the potential of digital technology to help educate and support GLBT communities, reflected on how his 'insider' status had facilitated his research:

Whilst the actual reference to, and disclosure of my own sexuality varies between interviews I find, during each interview, I use a number of non-heterosexual indicators or markers to inform the interviewees of my non-heterosexual identity. These markers operate in both subtle and explicit ways that act to indicate and reinforce my understanding of the subcultural knowledge of this community and my familiarity with the life experiences of the interviewees. For instance, this might include referring to common terms, acronyms and jargon that are familiar to this community. It also includes references to 'gay venues' and information and communication technologies (ICTs) that are targeted towards people who have non-heterosexual identities. Furthermore, it also includes acknowledgements of my familiarity with their life experiences of marginality and struggles, particularly around concerns of coming to terms with a non-heterosexual identity, or coming out to family and friends. As a non-heterosexual researcher my own narrative, and my familiarity of subcultural knowledge, affords me the opportunity to explore the interviewees' worlds in a different way than another researcher, with less connection to this community, might be able to. (Personal communication)

If you are not an insider it does necessarily preclude you doing research on the GLBT community. However, it may require significant commitment. McClennen (2003), who has done extensive qualitative research on domestic violence in the GLBT community, outlined how she went about doing this highly sensitive study despite being heterosexual. She followed the feminist participatory research model so as to overcome potential barriers. The model requires that the researcher gives 'voice to the members of the marginalized population' and breaks down hierarchy by incorporating the researched as much as possible in the framing of the study. A key strategy of McClennen's was to do voluntary work in the sector. Over time this allowed her to get to know the community and show her commitment and was crucial for her becoming trusted and accepted.

INTERVIEWING DISABLED PEOPLE

There is a good deal of contestation within the disability scholar community as to whether people who are abled should conduct qualitative research with disabled people (Kitchin, 2000). It has been argued that research on disability done by non-disabled researchers is necessarily limited as it is 'only disabled people who can truly interpret and present data from other disabled people' (Kitchin, 2000: 26). Oliver and Barnes (1997: 812) argue that although an impairment should not be 'a necessary prerequisite for doing disability research … the track record of non-disabled people doing disability research has not been noticeably successful.' For a non-disabled researcher doing disability research is challenging. It requires that the interviewer puts a good deal of effort into ensuring that they have the necessary background knowledge and adequate rapport with the interviewees. A key aspect in creating this rapport would be to use the research to advocate for disability rights. Tom Shakespeare (1996), who is disabled and a leading scholar in disability studies, outlines his interviewing method with disabled people.

> I explain exactly what the research is about; I give them the opportunity to revise what they have said and I offer them the opportunity to ask me questions, either about the research or about myself … I aim to equalise the research relationship and give participants some control over the process, over their words and over their participation. I try to be accountable to research participants, and I am committed to representing interviewees and giving them a voice within my publications. (1996: 116)

Again, the feminist participatory model is the guiding framework.

INTERVIEWS WITH SECOND LANGUAGE SPEAKERS

The increasing diversity of cities means that there is a substantial increase in the number of residents whose first language is not English. The interview is a crucial method for giving voice to immigrant groupings and presenting an account of their experiences. Ideally, interviews should be done in the language of the interviewee. However, this is not always possible. An interview conducted with a person whose first language is not English is certainly more open to misunderstanding. As Prior (2014) concludes,

> In cases where interviewers and interviewees do not share linguistic and cultural expertise … the risk of operating under competing assumptions, norms, and values is particularly high. (2014: 497)

What Prior is suggesting is that not only is there the possibility of slippage due to the interviewee not understanding or misinterpreting questions asked, but there also could be different conceptualisations of the research interview and how it should be conducted. In the interview situation it may take some time for these differences to reveal themselves and resolving these differences can be difficult. If an interviewee's English is limited it is likely that their answers may be too brief to use and/or may not reflect what they really think. Miller (2011) conducted three interviews with 'Peng', a Chinese immigrant, on his perceptions of discrimination. The first two interviews were conducted in English and the third in Mandarin.

Not surprisingly the third interview elicited far more detailed and nuanced answers (Miller, 2011: 53).

INTERVIEWING ELITES

Interviewing 'elites' presents a particular challenge. Elites can be defined as people in powerful positions in corporations, political parties, government or institutions. Invariably they have severe time constraints and will tend to have high expectations of the interviewer. Their position means that they usually have considerable power and control in their domain (and maybe beyond) and usually ask the questions rather than answer them. This can encourage an endeavour to control the interview by dominating the interaction or even by undermining the confidence and competence of the interviewer (King and Horrocks, 2012: 57). Interviewing an elite can be intimidating for a student and even an experienced researcher can find it anxiety provoking. A common problem when interviewing elites is a tendency to be deferential, daunted and tense. This can result in the interviewee dictating the interview and not giving you much opportunity to probe and/or to cover the relevant topics. Ideally, you need to appear confident, stand your ground and probe where necessary. Of course, a lot depends on who the interviewee is. Some elites will make an effort to create a relaxed, interactional situation.

What is imperative is that you are well prepared for the interview. You need to have a good knowledge of the subject matter and research the person you are going to interview. Biographical information is helpful. It will give you an idea of how to manage the interview. If an elite interviewee feels that you are not on top of the issues, it will impact on the quality of the interview (Richards, 1996: 201). Also, especially if you are interviewing ex or current politicians, you need to have a sense of whether they are 'twisting the truth'. Seldon (1988: 10) concludes that this group is particularly difficult to interview as they have great difficulties 'distinguishing the truth, so set have their minds become by long experience of partisan thought'. Oriana Fallaci, who during her career interviewed many of the world's leaders and is viewed as one of the greatest interviewers of all time, spent considerable time researching her interviewees prior to the actual interview (see Fallaci, 1976). Each of her interviews is preceded by a detailed essay on the interviewee and examines their politics and mindset. This intense preparation meant that she was able to pose the most astute and penetrating questions (Hitchens, 2006).

With elites it is worthwhile at the beginning of the interview to make it clear that they have the ability to decide which parts of the interview can be directly attributed and which cannot. The advantage of this approach is that it could encourage the interviewee to be more open and honest (Richards, 1996).

INTERVIEWING PEOPLE WHO ARE DISADVANTAGED AND MARGINALISED

On the other side of the spectrum, when an interviewee perceives that they have a lower status than the interviewer, there is a possibility that they could feel inhibited and give limited answers. They may fear that they will make a 'bad impression' or appear ignorant. Nairn et al. (2005) give the example of a 'failed' interview (focus group) with a group of Maori and Pacific Island students at a high school in New Zealand. The interview was a failure in that the responses of students were extremely brief. They argue that the,

> interviewer's embodiment [way of carrying herself] and her way of speaking (shaped by social class, age and geographic location) would have been interpreted by this group of students in a variety of ways, including the likely assumption that they could not relate to her, at least initially. (2005: 224–5)

In most cases a competent interviewer will be able to transcend a class and status divide and encourage rapport and a trusting relationship with the interviewee. When interviewing people on the margins it becomes even more important that you develop a good rapport with interviewees. It is crucial that you make them feel comfortable and indicate that you are interested in their life experiences and views. The choice of venue can take on added significance. For example, the interviewee may not feel comfortable being interviewed at a university and it may be more appropriate to conduct the interview in their own home and if this is not possible in a venue in which they feel comfortable. The way you couch and respond to questions is critical. You need to ensure that the language you use is accessible. In their research on how high school students in New Zealand perceive their rights, Nairn et al. (2005) concluded that a key reason for a group interview with Maori and Pacific Islander students eliciting little data and much laughter was that the students felt inhibited because of language difficulties. Also they did not feel the interview was being conducted in a 'safe space' (the school). They protected themselves by 'silence, laughing and other acts of resistance' (Nairn et al., 2005: 229).

In my own research I have found that people who are socially excluded and disadvantaged usually appreciate that a researcher is keen to know about their situation, experiences and perceptions. Of course, this is not always the case. If you are middle class, interviewees in a deprived neighbourhood may be suspicious of your middle class location and accent, and be dismissive of your research project. You may have to spend some time in the neighbourhood demonstrating your credentials and developing trust. If interviewees do not feel respected or understood they may decide to resist by giving partial or no answers to questions. Briggs (2003: 248–9) argues 'that respondents [interviewees] often attempt to resist discursive relations that are stacked against them' and that this is done by refusing to be cooperative. In his own research on Mexican Americans in New Mexico he tells of how initially the elderly respondents refused to divulge to the 'young gringo' and that only when he could illustrate his respect for this 'right to control the recontextualisation of discourse about the past' was he able to obtain information and insights.

SUMMARY

This chapter outlines the difficulties an interviewer may encounter and suggests possible ways to resolve them. Some problems are more difficult to resolve than others. There is only so much you can do if an interviewee refuses to sign the consent form or have the interview recorded. At times, interviewers can find themselves in unpredictable or even dangerous situations. The chapter makes suggestions as to how to lessen the risks if you are going into an unpredictable setting. Research on a highly sensitive topic is particularly challenging and requires a major effort by the interviewer to build the necessary rapport and trust and ask questions and probe in a manner that does not encourage resistance. The biggest and most common problem interviewers encounter is the interviewee who has little to say and as a consequence the interview data are not usable. In any study you are likely to encounter the odd reluctant interviewee. However, if most of your interviewees have little to say, you certainly have a problem. The chapter gives some suggestions as to how uncommunicative interviewees can be encouraged.

Interviewing across difference is a common feature of in-depth interviewing. The various key differences and challenges are discussed. Clearly, there are topics that should perhaps not be considered unless you have the attributes that will facilitate access and motivate interviewees to share their experiences. However, in many cases cross difference interviewing is possible. In some instances it will require you displaying a genuine commitment to the community that you are engaging. Interviewing elites is particularly challenging and thorough preparation is essential. Interviewing members of marginalised groupings presents a different challenge. Building rapport and trust are crucial in these studies.

Exercise

Dealing with difficulties and the unexpected

Go through your own or a colleague's transcript/s and note where there were unnecessary interruptions and where there could have been more adequate probing.

Reflecting on the two studies below reflect on how you would go about endeavouring to rescue an interview that is going badly.

Study 1: Why Indigenous young people are more likely to drop out of school'.

Study 2: 'How do HIV positive young men cope with their diagnosis?'

REFERENCES

Adamson, S. and Holloway, M. (2012) 'Negotiating sensitivities and grappling with intangibles: experiences from a study of spirituality and funerals', *Qualitative Research*, 12 (6): 735–55.

Belousov, K., Horlick-Jones, T., Bloor, M., Gilinskiy, Y., Golbert, V., Kostikovsky, Y., Levi, M. and Pentsov, D. (2007) 'Any port in a storm: fieldwork difficulties in dangerous and crisis-ridden settings', *Qualitative Research*, 7 (2): 155–75.

Bloor, M., Fincham, B. and Sampson, H. (2007) *Qualiti (NCRM) Commissioned Inquiry into the Risk to Well-being of Researchers in Qualitative Research*. Cardiff: ESRC National Centre for Research Methods.

Bohle, P., Quinian, M., Kennedy, D. and Williamson, A. (2004) 'Working hours, work-life conflict and health in precarious and "permanent" employment', *Rev Saúde Pública*, 38 (Supl): 19–25.

Briggs, C.L. (2003) 'Interviewing, power/knowledge and social inequality', in J.F. Gubrium and J.A. Holstein (eds), *Postmodern Interviewing*. Thousand Oaks, CA: SAGE. pp. 243–54.

Chatzifotiou, S. (2000) 'Conducting qualitative research on wife abuse: dealing with the issue of anxiety', *Sociological Research Online*, 5 (2). Available at: www.socresonline.org.uk/5/2/chatzifotiou.html, accessed 1 July 2014.

Clifford, J. (1986) 'Introduction: partial truths', in J. Clifford and G. Marcus (eds), *Writing Culture: The Poetics and Politics of Ethnography*. Berkeley: University of California Press. pp. 1–23.

Davis, D.W. (1997) The direction of race of interviewer effects among African-Americans: donning the black mask', *American Journal of Political Science*, 41 (1): 309–22.

Dyck, I. (1997) 'Dialogue with difference: a tale of two studies', in S. Roberts, H. Nast and J.P. Jones III (eds), *Thresholds in Feminist Geography*, Lanham, MD: Rowman and Littlefield. pp. 183–202.

Fallaci, O. (1976) *Interview with History*. London: Joseph.

Fletcher, C. (2003) 'Community-based participatory research relationships with Aboriginal communities in Canada: an overview of context and process', *Pimatisiwin: A Journal of Aboriginal & Indigenous Community Health*, 1 (1): 27–63.

Fontana, A. and Frey, J. H. (2008) 'The interview: from neutral stance to political involvement', in N. K. Denzin and Y. S. Lincoln (eds), *Collecting and Interpreting Qualitative Materials*, London: SAGE. pp. 115–60.

Hitchens, C. (2006) 'Oriana Fallaci and the art of the interview', *Vanity Fair*, December. Available at: www.vanityfair.com/politics/features/2006/12/hitchens200612, accessed 2 August 2014.

Howell, N. (1990) *Surviving Fieldwork*. Report of the Advisory Panel on Health and Safety in Fieldwork, Washington DC: American Anthropological Association.

Hunter, E. (2001) 'A brief historical background to health research in indigenous communities', *Aboriginal and Islander Health Worker Journal*, 25 (1): 6–8.

Johnson-Bailey, J. (1999) 'The ties that bind and the shackles that separate: race, gender, class, and colour in a research process', *International Journal of Qualitative Studies in Education*, 12 (6): 659–70.

Kenny, C. (2004) *A Holistic Framework for Aboriginal Policy Research*, Ottawa: Research Directorate, Status of Women, Canada.

King, N. and Horrocks, C. (2012) *Interviews in Qualitative Research*. London: SAGE.

Kitchin, R. (2000) 'The researched opinions on research: disabled people and disability research', *Disability & Society*, 15 (1): 25–47.

LaSala, M.C. (2003) 'When interviewing "family": maximising the insider advantage in the qualitative study of lesbians and gay men', *Journal of Gay & Lesbian Social Services*, 15 (1–2): 15–30.

Lee, R.M. (1995) *Dangerous Fieldwork*. Qualitative Research Methods Series 34. London: SAGE.

Lee, Y-O. and Lee, R.M. (2012) 'Methodological research on "sensitive" topics: a decade review', *Bulletin de Methodologie Sociologique*, 114 (1): 35–49.

Lowe, S.R., Lustig, K. and Marrow, H.B. (2011) 'African American women's reports of racism during Hurricane Katrina: variation by interviewer race', *New School Psychological Bulletin*, 8 (2): 46–57.

Marks, M. (2001) *Young Warriors: Youth Politics, Identity and Violence in South Africa*. Johannesburg: Witwatersrand University Press.

McClennen, J.C. (2003) 'Researching gay and lesbian domestic violence; the journey of a non-LGBT researcher', *Journal of Gay & Lesbian Social Services*, 15 (1–2): 31–45.

Meadows, L.M., Lagendyk, L.E., Thurston, W.E. and Eisener, A.C. (2003) 'Balancing culture, ethics, and methods in qualitative health research with Aboriginal peoples', *International Institute for Qualitative Methodology*, 2 (4): 1–14.

Meezan, W. and Martin, J.I. (2003) 'Exploring current themes in research on gay, lesbian, bisexual and transgender populations', *Gay & Lesbian Social Services*, 15 (1–2): 1–14.

Miller, K.R. (2011) 'Indeterminacy and interviewer research: co-constructing ambiguity and clarity in interviews with an adult immigrant learner of English', *Applied Linguistics*, 32 (1): 43–59.

Morris, A. (1999) *Bleakness & Light: Inner-City Transition in Hillbrow, Johannesburg*. Johannesburg. Witwatersrand University Press.

Nairn, K., Munro, J. and Smith, A.B. (2005) 'A counter-narrative of a "failed" interview', *Qualitative Research*, 5 (2): 221–44.

Oakley, A. (1981) 'Interviewing women: a contradiction in terms', in H. Roberts (ed.), *Doing Feminist Research*. Boston: Routledge. pp: 30–61.

Oliver, M. and Barnes, C. (1997) 'All we are saying is give disabled researchers a chance', *Disability & Society*, 12 (5): 811–14.

Prior, M. (2014) 'Re-examining alignment in a "failed" L2 autobiographic research interview', *Qualitative Inquiry*, 20 (4): 495–508.

Reinharz, S., and Chase, S. E. (2001) 'Interviewing women', in J. F. Gubrium and J. A. Holstein (eds), *The Handbook of Interview Research: Context and Method*. Thousand Oaks, CA: SAGE. pp. 221–38.

Rhodes, P.J. (1994) 'Race-of-interviewer effects: a brief comment', *Sociology*, 28 (2): 547–58.

Richards, D. (1996) 'Elite interviewing: approaches and pitfalls', *Politics*, 16 (3): 199–204.

Roulston, K. (2011) 'Interview "problems" as topics for analysis', *Applied Linguistics*, 32 (1): 77–94.

Rubin, H.J. and Rubin, I.S. (1995) *Qualitative Interviewing: The Art of Hearing Data*. Thousand Oaks, CA: SAGE.

Sampson, H. and Thomas, H. (2003) 'Risk and responsibility', *Qualitative Research*, 3 (2): 165–89.

Seldon, A. (ed) (1988) *Contemporary History*. New York: Basil Blackwell.

Shakespeare, T. (1996) 'Rules of engagement: doing disability research', *Disability & Society*, 11 (1): 115–21.

Smith, L.T. (2001) 'Troubling spaces', *International Journal of Critical Psychology*, 4 (2): 167–82.

Stroebe, M., Stroebe, W. and Schut, H. (2003) 'Bereavement research: methodological issues and ethical concerns', *Palliative Medicine*, 17: 235–40.

Tixier y Vigil, Y. and Elsasser, N. (1978) 'The effects of the interviewer on conversation: a study of Chicana women', *International Journal of the Sociology of Language*, 17, 91–102.

Wasserfall, R. (1993) 'Reflexivity, feminism and difference', *Qualitative Sociology*, 16 (1): 23–41.

8

TRANSCRIBING, ANALYSING AND WRITING UP THE INTERVIEWS

A major challenge is the translation of your interviews into a coherent, interesting and convincing academic piece of writing. The conversion of a substantial amount of interview text into an adequate academic article, chapter or thesis requires patience, creativity, organisation and a clear notion of the research questions you are trying to answer. This chapter goes through the key features of translating transcripts into articles/chapters. Chapter headings include:

- Transcribing the interview
- Crucial – adequate storing and labelling of your interviews and consent forms
- Analysing the interviews – the question of how to view the interview data
- When to start analysing the transcripts
- Analysing the transcripts
- Vignettes
- Coding and the use of software programs to organise interview data
- Recommended websites for QDA software

TRANSCRIBING THE INTERVIEW

Once you have completed an interview, the next step is to transcribe it. This is a skilled, time-consuming and, if you outsource the task, costly exercise. It is an essential part of the research process. Accurate transcripts are required for analysing the interview data and in most instances it is preferable to quote the exact words of your interviewees. You should not 'correct' the language of the interviewee. Often, it may be grammatically incorrect but rich in meaning and imagery. If you 'tidy' it up you risk losing the richness of the language used. If you transcribe the interviews yourself you should date the interview and give the biographical details of the interviewee at the beginning – their age, sex, where they live if pertinent, employment if appropriate, marital status, education and any other biographical and contextual information. Alternatively, you can insert this information when you get the transcript back from the transcriber. These demographic/biographical data are useful for when you write up the interviews. You want to be able to give the reader a profile of the interviewee being quoted or spoken about. Ideally, you should record this information just before the start of the interview. Of course, in the write-up you need to be careful not to identify participants.

Preferably you should transcribe the interviews yourself. Besides the financial saving, it intimately acquaints you with the material, gives you the opportunity to assess where the gaps are and you can gauge where and how your interviewing technique was wanting and can be improved (Ezzy, 2002: 70). Another advantage of transcribing yourself is that you can leave out material that is not pertinent and add comments where appropriate about how the interviewee responded to particular questions – 'she appeared agitated'; 'she thought this was very funny'; 'laughed cynically', etc. You can also describe body language. A disadvantage of you transcribing, is that it is a time-consuming activity and you may not do a good job. If you are not a particularly fast typist, an hour interview could take you up to eight hours to transcribe. If you are not experienced you may miss detail. In their study of 15 PhD students who each transcribed the interviews they conducted, Roulston et al. (2003: 657) found that the quality of the transcribing varied significantly: 'Although some students provided close and detailed transcriptions … others missed sections of talk'.

Transcribing is a lot easier when the recording is clear. You need to make sure that your equipment is in good working order and appropriately placed during the interview (see Chapter 5). If the digital voice recorder is too far from the interviewee the recording may be inaudible in certain places. If the interviewee is a 'soft-talker', encourage them to speak a bit louder and move the recorder closer.

It is important to keep an accurate record of when and where the interview was conducted and note any other aspects that may be relevant. A useful exercise is to note the quality of the interview out of 10 and make a comment. A record, like the one suggested (see Table 8.1), can be extremely useful, especially when you come back to interviews that you did a while back; it is difficult to remember an interview that you did a year ago. However, if you gave it a mark of 10 out of 10 you know that it is a quality interview that you need to give close attention. Table 8.1 is a suggested table for record keeping.

Table 8.1 *Profile of older renters interviewed*

Name of interviewee	Date of the interview	Location	Quality of interview out of 10	Any other comments
Michael Smith	23/11/2012	Surry Hills	5	Very ordinary interview. Interviewee had little to say.
Paul Fielding	01/03/2014	Waterloo	8	Very good interview. Has been in the private renter sector (PRS) since his divorce in 1993.
Francis Roux	28/09/2013	Kingsford	8	Very good interview. Became a private renter after business went into liquidation.
Mary King	04/08/2013	Orange	9	A lot of detail given about what it's like living on the age pension and being a private renter.
Susan Miller	12/09/2013	Penrith	6	Generally a very ordinary interview. A couple of interesting points.
Janet Bruce	07/11/2013	Maroubra	7	Had interesting things to say about relationship with landlord.
Michelle McNeil	16/06/2013	Auburn	3	This was a weak interview. Interviewee could not be drawn.
Rita Haywood	02/04/2014	Kingsgrove	10	Interviewee has been a private renter for over 20 years. Had some superb insights and stories.
Rod Williams	25/05/2014	Kingsgrove	9	His depiction of the health impacts of living on the age pension and being in the PRS were disturbing.

Seidman's (2013) observation is certainly excellent advice:

> Although there is no one right way to organise the research process and the materials it generates, every moment the researcher spends paying attention to order, labels, filing, and documentation at the beginning and in the formative stages of the study can save hours of frustration later. (2013: 115)

CRUCIAL – ADEQUATE STORING AND LABELLING OF YOUR INTERVIEWS AND CONSENT FORMS

It is essential that you store your recordings and transcripts in a safe place. Many organisations have regulations in place as to how research data should be stored and you need to be aware of these (see Chapter 2). If data go astray, for example if you lose a USB stick with a number of interview transcripts, this can have serious implications, especially if the transcripts have not been deidentified.

On your personal computer you should develop a precise system for storing the transcripts. If you are in an organisation where there is a shared drive you need to ensure that access to the transcripts is adequately password protected and that only you can access them.

ANALYSING THE INTERVIEWS – THE QUESTION OF HOW TO VIEW THE INTERVIEW DATA

How to view and analyse the interview material is contentious and is dependent on your methodological and philosophical approach. Rapley (2001) has succinctly summarised the different perspectives on approaching interview data:

> *Interview-data-as-resource*: the interview data collected are seen as (more or less) reflecting the interviewee's reality outside the interview.
>
> *Interview-data-as-topic*: the interview data collected are seen as (more or less) reflecting a reality jointly constructed by the interviewee and the interviewer. (2001: 304)

If you accept the former approach the implication is that responses of interviewees can be analysed without having to reflect on the interview itself. What the interviewer says in response to questions is accepted as a valid and accurate reflection of their social reality.

The second position (the constructionist position) argues that what the interviewee says in the interview cannot be analysed on the basis that the interview data necessarily reflect the interviewee's world. The constructionist position presents the researcher with a dilemma. If the data cannot be accepted as reflecting the reality of the interviewee, how do we go about analysing the data collected? The constructionist approach argues that all we can do is analyse the interview itself – 'interviews merely report upon, or express, their own structures' (Rapley, 2001: 307).

A compromise position is where the interviewer approaches the interview material reflexively. Whatever position you take you need to be aware of the interview as a co-construction. This position entails taking note of the talk of both the interviewee and the interviewer, the argument being that the setting and interviewer play a central role in shaping the responses of the interviewee and that the interview itself is a particular kind of forum and interaction. In the interview, the interviewee may present recounts of their experiences and views that might be different to what they would present to friends, family or another interviewee. They will usually endeavour to present themselves in a favourable light or what Rapley calls a 'morally adequate light'. This may involve highlighting some material and omitting content that may be too painful or revealing. This certainly does not mean that in-depth interviewing is a fruitless method, rather it means that at the very least when you analyse your interviews you should contextualise the interviewee's answers and take account of the question that prompted the response. If you are interviewing across difference this could be significant and you need to reflect on the possible implications.

The focus in this chapter is on thematic approaches to analysing interviews. This is probably the most common approach and is premised on the notion that what the interviewee says does reflect their world to a greater or lesser extent. Of course, interviewees will exaggerate certain aspects, omit important information and distort 'reality', but nevertheless, in most cases, interviewees, if they feel comfortable, do endeavour to answer questions as honestly as their memory allows. This is the position I am taking in this chapter. If you are interested in alternatives to the thematic approach, Kvale and Brinkmann (2009) give an excellent overview of the different approaches to analysing interviews.

WHEN TO START ANALYSING THE TRANSCRIPTS

Should you analyse the interview transcripts as they come in or should you wait until you have completed all of the interviews? Personally, I think it is good practice to start analysing the interviews as they come in. It is partially a practical issue. Depending on the project there is often a good deal of time between the first and the last interview and if this is your major research project and you have time constraints it is probably not a good idea to wait until all the interviews are in. More importantly, when you start analysing your interviews you can rapidly obtain an idea of what the issues are and what you may have missed asking in the initial interviews (see Miles and Huberman, 1994). Early analysis gives you the opportunity to refine your interview guide and focus on aspects you may not have thought of in the initial interviews and/or on unexpected issues that have emerged (Ezzy, 2002: 61). There is a contrary view. Seidman (2013: 116) advocates that you should complete all your interviews before you start the in-depth analysis so as 'to avoid imposing meaning from one participant's interviews on the next'. This does appear to be an ultra-cautious approach.

ANALYSING THE TRANSCRIPTS

Analysing interview material is a time-consuming and challenging task. Even if you do 20 interviews you could have around 400 pages of text to analyse and convert into a document that answers the research question/s you have been investigating in a clear, 'accurate', comprehensive and readable fashion. Selections have to be made. However, what to select and how to analyse the data is wide open. Miles (1979) captures the dilemma of the social scientist who uses in-depth interviews or other qualitative methods:

> But the most serious and central difficulty in the use of qualitative data is that methods of analysis are not well formulated. For quantitative data, there are clear conventions the researcher can use. But the analyst faced with a bank of qualitative data has very few guidelines for protection against self-delusion, let alone the presentation of 'unreliable' or 'invalid' conclusions to scientific or policy-making audiences. How can we be sure that an 'earthy', 'undeniable', 'serendipitous' finding is not, in fact, *wrong*? (1979: 591)

Miles' statement is perhaps too strong. However, there is no doubt that there is not one way or a 'correct' way of analysing interviews. As Kvale and Brinkmann (2009: 233) conclude, most researchers reliant on in-depth interviews for their data use 'a multiplicity of ad hoc methods and conceptual approaches' in their analysis. However, despite the absence of a definitive approach there are guidelines that, if taken on board, can certainly facilitate the task. I have identified five stages for analysing the interview data. They are not necessarily bounded and there will be overlap.

Stage 1 – The careful read-through and note-taking

It is highly recommended that you read through all your transcripts carefully without the distraction of worrying about coding. You should make notes about each interview in regards to its overall quality and the key aspects that emerged. Every interview is different – interviewees focus on different aspects. This initial reading should immerse you in the data and give you a good sense of what are the important themes. One thorough reading is often not enough. In her article on analysing interviews, Appleton (1995: 995) describes how she 'listened to each tape, transcribed each tape herself and then read each transcript several times in order to familiarise herself with the data.'

Stage 2 – Notable quotes

It is useful to have a file that is constituted by what Rubin and Rubin (2012: 195) call 'notable quotes'. Your notable quote file will be made up of striking quotes that capture key points/themes. Stages 1 and 2 can be merged to save time. Notable quotes will include quotes which express strong feelings about a particular issue or which, through the use of imagery and metaphor, powerfully capture a particular sentiment. The following extract from an interview with a 72-year-old public housing tenant, powerfully captures the way having affordable, adequate and secure (secure in the sense of not having to be worried about having to move) housing, is foundational for leading a decent life while dependent on a government age pension for income:

> Interviewee: Well I was getting older and ... you know the rent [in the private rental sector] sort of was going up all the time and I just felt that I wanted a little bit of security and I knew a few people in public housing and they seemed to be quite satisfied so I more or less pursued that angle ... There is a certain feeling of security when you've got the Department of Housing here and so on and so forth. So that's the main reason ... Landlords can always put up their rent and I found that the Government is the best landlord that I've ever had. They're very responsive. They leave you alone and as long as you pay the rent, they don't interfere ... I do feel that there is a terrific lot of security here. It makes for a far more peaceful life especially when you get older, when people get older as you know they sort of become easily stressed and the accommodation is probably at the top of the list.

Quotes that reflect conflict are usually of interest as are those that are surprising and reveal something you had not thought about. Interesting quotes that go against the expected should also be noted.

Stage 3 – Coding/finding the themes

Once you have read through all your interviews and have got a feel for the content you need to code the interviews. The coding process is analogous to organising the interview material into themes, it allows you to compare the responses of inter-viewees and is a crucial part of making sense of the interviews and converting the interviews into a meaningful, coherent analysis. It requires a careful reading of the transcripts and will also be guided by your interview guide. If you are coding the hard copy and not using a software program you can develop your own method of coding. Once you have identified the themes you can colour code each theme on the actual hard copies of the transcripts. Alternatively, each quote that corresponds to a particular theme can be transferred to an appropriate file on your computer.

The choosing of themes should not be too challenging. Ultimately the themes you select should reflect what you think are the important and salient topics and associated data required to answer the research question/s posed. Interview mate-rial that is strong and powerful invariably reveals itself. You need to look for those powerful, illuminating accounts. Repetition is another important aspect of a theme. If one or two interviewees mention an issue, it may be interesting but does not really qualify as a theme (King and Horrocks, 2012: 149). Of course, it could be interesting to examine why an interviewee is going against the trend. Another feature of a theme noted by King and Horrocks (2012) is that ideally they should be distinct; there should not be too much overlap.

You need to approach the interview material with an open mind. Strong pre-conceptions of what the data should be telling you could result in the overlooking or underplaying of important material that undermines your position. Social real-ity is messy and it is important to look for common themes and contradictory accounts and perceptions and try and work out how these contradictory accounts can be explained. For example, two older private renters who are using a similar proportion of their income to pay for their accommodation may have very differ-ent accounts of the impact. Interviewee 1 may have no resources to partake in leisure activities and feel perpetually anxious about their situation. In contrast, interviewee 2 is socially engaged and has a positive outlook. If you look at the interviews you may find that interviewee 1 has limited or no family support whereas interviewee 2 may have significant family support. The latter may be the key factor in regards to an older private renter's capacity to lead a decent life. This is illustrated in the case of Jeanette and Rod (not their real names). Jeanette had a good deal of family support whilst Rod was relatively isolated. It was evident that Jeanette's disposition and capacity to live a decent life was far greater than Rod's. Jeanette described her family situation in the following way:

> Yes, it is [difficult surviving on the age pension], but … I've got my two daughters … and they said, 'If ever you need anything, any bills to be paid just ask'. And when she found out you know, she said, 'You should get a computer', and I said, 'Ah no. I'm not interested'. Well she got me one.

She also relied on her sister who lived in a comfortable middle-class situation: 'Ah yes, I've got my sister … Well I go to her place every Saturday and Sunday. We spend the weekend. It's quite good.' Her grandson supplied her with fish:

> So I'm lucky there. Every time, if I'm going down there [down to the coast to visit one of her daughters] at the weekend, well he'll get all the fish that he's caught and he'll take it into the co-op and they will snap freeze it for him and I bring it home.

In contrast, Rod had to rely on his own resources.

> Yes, it is stressful … I have two daughters and one I don't have anything to do with really, … but my other daughter … she's been supportive in as much as she can … but I have three grandchildren and I don't want to impact on their education and as luck would have it, my son-in-law who is [unemployed] … You know I can't expect them to support me.

In the case of older social housing tenants family support was important, but the interviews indicated that the key issues shaping their capacity to lead a decent life was the fixed low rent and guaranteed security of tenure. This is evident from Dorothy's experience. When she was interviewed, Dorothy was 85 and leading an active life:

> I understand that well the rent's very good here. I pay $120 a fortnight but there's water in that. I'm always ahead of me rent; always four weeks ahead … I'd never be able to live if I had to go out private. I look at it that way.

Margaret, who had recently managed to obtain a place in social housing after a spell in the private rental sector, described the impact of having secure, affordable housing:

> Yeah. I've sort of relaxed here. I'm a different person. At least you've got a roof over your head and you know that you're not going to be thrown out … In private rental it's a worry all the time. It really is …

Usually, there will be a close match between your interview guide and the themes as the questions asked will be shaped by the guide. If we go back to the interview guide on older private renters discussed in Chapter 3, we can gauge how the interview guide can form the basis for the coding of themes. The interview guide had the following themes: History of becoming a private renter; the adequacy of the accommodation; the cost of the accommodation and its impact; finances/budgeting; landlord–tenant relationship/maintenance; health; the neighbourhood; leisure and social connections; social and family support; housing options and policy; and the future.

The list of 11 themes is not an exhaustive list. For example, theme four, finances/budgeting can be divided into various sub-themes: shopping for food; ability to look after one's health; ability to replace essential items and use of charity. Similarly, the theme on the neighbourhood may also have a number of sub-themes: neighbours; services; friends; noise issues; safety and security; and sense of community. Themes may overlap. Thus there may be a good deal of crossover between the neighbourhood and the leisure and social connection themes. The latter will certainly include friends and probably neighbours.

For an extensive and excellent analysis of the different kinds of coding in qualitative research the review by Saldana (2012) is recommended.

Stage 4 – Selecting the themes you are going to focus on when writing up the interviews

When you have completed the coding exercise you should be in a position to make decisions as to what to focus on. Not all themes will be of equivalent importance and in the course of the interviews it is likely that a couple of dominant themes will emerge. A key criterion is the richness of the data on a particular theme. If a number of interviewees have passionately spoken about a particular issue this suggests that you should take it further in the write-up. Interview talk that goes against the dominant trend should also be considered; you need to explain these contrary perceptions and concerns. If there are particular research questions you are focusing on, you will want to focus on those themes that will help you answer these research questions.

The existing research on the topic should also play a role in your theme selection. For example, if your primary research question is 'what impact has the decline of manufacturing had on young working class males?' you would need to consult some of the key studies in this area (Connell, 1995; McDowell, 2003; Weis, 1990; Wilson, 1996) so that you can engage with the existing research and illustrate how your interviews accord with or challenge existing analyses. You may want to look at the issues of identity construction (Connell, 1995; McDowell, 2003), employment (Wilson, 1996) and perceptions of school and schooling (McDowell, 2003; Weis, 1990). These could all be key themes.

Stage 5 – Interpreting and writing up the interview data, drawing on the themes identified

The interview data will help you describe the phenomenon you are focusing on, however, you also want to explain or interpret the interview material. Seidman (2013) proposes a number of useful questions that you should pose around analysing the data:

Researchers must ask themselves what they have learned from doing the interviews, studying the transcripts, marking and labelling them … What connective threads are there among the experiences of the participants they interviewed? How do they understand and explain these connections? What do they understand now that they did not understand before they began the interviews? What surprises have there been? What confirmations of previous instincts? How have their interviews been consistent with the literature? How inconsistent? How have they gone beyond? (2013: 130)

The question of connective threads is important. You need to ask what were common themes in the interviews. In the study I did with a colleague on the life circumstances of people who were dependent on the government unemployment benefit (Newstart) for their income (Morris and Wilson, 2014), there were a number of common themes. It was evident that the capabilities of almost all of the interviewees were severely constrained by a lack of financial resources. Another common theme was that the longer people were on the unemployment benefit, the greater their level of desperation. This was explained by the depletion of savings and an intensification of psychological stress (scarring) as the prospect of long-term or even permanent unemployment became a possibility. Not surprisingly, another important connecting theme was that interviewees who were living by themselves were usually far more vulnerable. What the interviews illustrated – we only had an inkling of this prior to the interviews – was how totally counterproductive the low unemployment benefit is. The low payment is presented by the government as an incentive for recipients to find employment, however what the interviews indicated was that the low payment made it a lot harder for people to re-enter the world of work. This was keenly captured by one of the interviewees.

Interviewee: And so … $260 a week, … is completely insufficient financially to live a normal healthy existence *and* look for work. By that I mean maintain interview clothes … appearance and health that is going to be acceptable at an interview situation; pay for transport, rent, electricity, phone, food for example. There's simply not enough money. … Putting someone on a drip feed of $20 a week is not going to do anything for them. Whereas if I could have continued on [a decent income] I would have found another job within months … Sometimes I've had to walk to interviews, like kilometres, without a cent in my pocket, and hungry. This is a system that is unfortunately, so self-perpetuating …

You should identify what King and Horrocks (2012) have called overarching themes. An overarching theme could be a concept that captures the situation of most interviewees. In our study of Newstart recipients an overarching theme was the concept of 'scarring', the notion that unemployment had a major impact on well-being (Clark et al., 2001).

The strength of your analysis will to a large extent depend on the quality of your interview data. As Rubin and Rubin (2012) note,

> No matter how far you take your analysis, you always need to have ample and explicit evidence in your interviews to back up every conclusion. That evidence provides the basis for writing a convincing report. (2012: 211)

What is crucial is that in your writing up you answer the research question/s using your interview material in a clear, coherent and imaginative fashion and, where possible, explain your findings, drawing on existing research, concepts and theoretical approaches. The quotes you choose should 'highlight the nature of the theme vividly, ... [be] easily understood and, where possible, give some sense of the character of the speaker ...' (King and Horrocks, 2012: 165).

A key premise is that your write-up should reflect your interview material. It is not acceptable to deliberately ignore interview material that does not substantiate the argument you are making. Although the process of quotes selection is ultimately subjective, and you cannot deal with all the ambiguities that are a necessary part of social reality, where things are murky and not clear-cut, you should make this clear to the reader. Social reality is complex and there will always be some uncertainty so you need to present your findings with some degree of hedging. There is no doubt that in some quarters qualitative research is still viewed with some scepticism; Kvale and Brinkmann (2009) conclude that it is ultimately up to the researcher to persuade their audience through their evident craftsmanship:

> Ideally, the quality of the craftsmanship results in products with knowledge claims that are so powerful and convincing in their own right that they, so to say, carry the validation with them, like a strong piece of art. In such cases, the research procedures would be transparent and the results evident, and the conclusions of a study intrinsically convincing as true, beautiful, and good. (2009: 260)

A potential problem with the write-up of interviews is that it can be 'deadly for the reader'. If you present a string of quotes with minimal interpretation there is a strong possibility that the reader will find it dry and tedious. Ideally, you should aim to present new, interesting knowledge that engages with relevant theoretical material and consider whether your findings accord with or question existing research. You also need to satisfy the reader that your findings and interpretation are valid. This requires that you give the reader a clear account of how you went about gathering your data.

Although there is no standard way of presenting interview material or set rules, there are some things you should bear in mind. The guide below partially draws on the useful summary by Kvale and Brinkmann (2009: 279–81).

- Unless you are presenting a profile/story (see below), a quote should normally not be too long. Kvale and Brinkmann (2009) suggest half a page maximum. Short quotes, less than 30 words, often do not tell us much. Although there is no definitive guide, it is usually better to use longer quotes – 50 words plus, around three sentences, is a good minimum.
- You should contextualise the quote. Where appropriate, the reader should be told what question prompted the answer given.
- Do not just present a quote, but interpret what it illustrates. The reader needs to know why you have selected a particular quote.
- There should be a balance between text and the quotes. It has been argued that the quotes should not constitute more than half of the text in the write-up (Kvale and Brinkmann, 2009: 280).
- When there is a range of views you should try and capture these using quotes. Where there is broad agreement a couple of key quotes may suffice.
- Where necessary edit the quote by adding words in square brackets or by deleting words. The latter should be indicated by '...' (an ellipsis). There is little point having quotes that are difficult to understand. However, ideally you should use the actual words of the interviewee.
- If possible, draw out the theoretical implications of the interview data.
- Discuss how your interview material confirms or contradicts existing theory and research.
- Where appropriate and possible use concepts to try and explain your findings.
- Try and explain interview material that contradicts dominant trends/patterns in the interviews.
- Organise the write-up under headings.
- Introduction of dialogue can be a useful device for adding interest and variety.
- Vignettes/profiles can make for compelling reading.
- Tell the reader how the interview knowledge was produced. The way the data were collected should be made evident.
- Remember to respect confidentiality. Pseudonyms are essential and where necessary change the names of places.
- In the process of writing up your interviews you will have to let go a substantial amount of interview material. This can be a painful process but is an inevitable part of the analysis.

VIGNETTES

A vignette using the words of the interviewee is a powerful way of sharing data. It gives the reader a fuller picture and allows you to give the context and explain their experiences. The actual words of the interviewee should be used as much as possible; the first person is far more powerful than the third person (Seidman, 2013).

Below is a short vignette from an interview I conducted with an older renter, here referred to as Kevin. It powerfully illustrates the impact of being dependent on the age pension and not having access to affordable and adequate accommodation. The struggles of Kevin are disturbing and poignant as he describes how the lack of affordable housing forced him to leave a vibrant neighbourhood in Sydney where he had lived for most of his life and move to a small remote village where he knew no one. After his de facto partner died, her daughter told him that he would have to now pay a market rent.

Kevin's story

And the rent was going to be put up from … $110 to $500 and that was the decision I had to make was to move from Sydney … because there was no possible way I could have stayed in Sydney and paid the rent …

I had a look around; … I even went to places, rooms to rent in Canterbury [a suburb in Sydney]. They started from $165. You wouldn't have stayed there one night. They were that bad and that was from $165 per room … Absolutely terrible. There was nothing in it. There was one old wardrobe that would have been 50 years old and that was it. There was no way that you could put all your furniture into that room. Shared sort of kitchenette and the rest of it was shared too, bathroom and so depressing. I just had to get out immediately … and then on me walks I'd see these poor [homeless] chaps in the park. I thought no wonder they're laying in the parks. Even on pensions or whatever they got off the government they could not have even got a room.

It was so desperate that I went down with a heart thing and I was rushed to hospital and I was operated on and I never woke up for three days. That was the pressure that you're under. It's like a pressure cooker. You don't know where to go, what to do and it was only then that I thought, 'Well I can't afford Sydney. I must have to look over the mountains', and that's how I ended up in …

I went to the Department of Housing and I was sitting in there and they said, 'Where would you like to go?' 'Well', I said, 'You're not offering me anything in Sydney.' I said, 'I can understand that because of the accommodation how hard it is' and they said, 'Where would you like to go?' I didn't really know. I said, 'Wagga [a regional town] or anything you know', but they … could not offer me anything and they knew that I had to get out [of Sydney] …

It's a terrible thing and the … bug of living in rural areas there's no [adequate] medical, … no transport. You can get out of the area once a week and that's for three hours in Wagga but you miss that 3.45 bus back that's it. There's no way out. You can't get back.

In Sydney I had my friends that lived opposite me … Very nice people and ones next to them. They were near crying when they knew I had to move out and it was lovely to have had friends like that … When I moved up here I didn't know a soul. It was hard, but I thought at least I've got a roof over my head. I can afford the food and that but you are isolated. There's no doubt about it. Yes. It's a bit lonely you know. I mean at 72 and that there's not a great deal to do. They've got a little pub around the corner but there's not much doing there at all, No card games or anything like that.

CODING AND THE USE OF SOFTWARE PROGRAMS TO ORGANISE INTERVIEW DATA

If you are conducting a number of interviews it is certainly worth considering using computer-assisted qualitative data analysis software (CAQDAS). Programs like NVivo, MaxQDA and ATLAs are designed to make it easier for you to manage a large amount of interview data (Seale and Rivas, 2012). CAQDAS has several useful features. You can store all your interviews. The capacity to create a profile of interviewees is useful. The most useful function is that you are able to code and organise the data in a relatively rapid fashion: 'They replace the time-consuming "cut and paste" approach to hundreds of pages of transcripts with electronic scissors' (Kvale and Brinkmann, 2009: 198). You can assign the same material to different codes and then retrieve data under the particular codes. There is also the capacity to quantify qualitative data: 'CAQDAS packages may also enable the incorporation of quantitative (numeric) data and/tools for taking quantitative approaches to qualitative data' (Lewins and Silver, 2009 in Humble, 2012: 123).

In my own research I use a combination of hard copy and NVivo (this is not to suggest that NVivo is necessarily superior to any of the other CAQDAS packages). NVivo has what it calls primary and secondary nodes. The primary node is the main theme and the secondary nodes are the sub-themes. In the course of my research with older private renters I developed the following coding structure. The primary nodes were history of becoming a private renter; adequacy of accommodation; rent paid and its impact; expenditure and budget; health impacts; landlord–tenant relations; social and family support; the difficulties of moving; the insecurity of being a private renter; and policy suggestions.

Under each of these primary nodes I had secondary nodes. For example, under *adequacy of accommodation* I had: description of accommodation; condition; age; friendliness; and safety. Under *expenditure and budget* I had: coping strategies; difficulty of paying rent; financial stress; food costs and ability to consume adequately; running a car; ability to access public transport; unexpected expenses/ability to replace appliances; and energy costs. Under *neighbourhood* the sub-nodes were: friends; neighbours; infrastructure; noise issues; safety; sense of community; and services. For *landlord–tenant relations* the sub-nodes were: maintenance; rent increases; bad landlord behaviour; and insecurity.

As mentioned, having a 'notable quote file' (Rubin and Rubin, 2012) or node is highly recommended. These quotes would capture key sentiments, experiences and views.

Although I use NVivo, I always go back to reading through the transcripts. I tend to see things that I would miss in the fragmented world of NVivo. It is evident that for some qualitative researchers, CAQDAS is effectively used. However, there are limitations. Ultimately it is you who has to do the coding and the analysis; CAQDAS cannot do it for you.

RECOMMENDED WEBSITES FOR QDA SOFTWARE

- www.qsrinternational.com/products_nvivo.aspx?utm_source=NVivo+10+for+Mac
- www.maxqda.com
- www.atlasti.com/index.html
- http://provalisresearch.com/products/qualitative-data-analysis-software

If you cannot afford CAQDAS, some applications have a 30-day free trial. Others have a version that is free. For example QDA Miner has a free version of their software called QDA Miner Lite.

WEFT QDA is an open access free software package for analysing interviewing. www.pressure.to/qda/

SUMMARY

This chapter examines the complex task of translating in-depth interviews into a lively and credible academic publication. Precise transcription of interviews is a key part of the process. Transcribing the interviews yourself allows you to immerse yourself in the interview material from the start and gives you the opportunity to add commentary to the text. However, it is time-consuming, and accurate transcription requires a fair amount of skill. The question of when to start analysing the transcripts has caused some debate. I argue that you should start from the first interview as early analysis will give you the capacity to gauge what questions you should have asked but did not, and what issues are emerging. A major debate shaping analyses of interview material is how the interview material is viewed. Should the interview data be viewed as reflecting the interviewer's reality, or as a reality jointly constructed by the interviewer and the interviewee? Clearly, the interview material is a co-construction of the interviewer and interviewee, however this does not preclude you analysing the interview material and reaching conclusions about the social reality of the interviewees. It is essential that you approach the interview material reflexively and be alert to how the interview itself and the setting have shaped the 'interview talk'. Although there are no hard and fast rules for analysing interview material beyond the basic maxim that you should do your best to ensure that the write-up reflects the world of the interviewees, there are certain procedures you can adopt to increase the effectiveness of your analysis. Five stages are identified. The first stage requires a careful reading of the transcript at least once. In this close reading you should note the key issues that emerge. The second stage can be merged with stage one and involves the noting of notable quotes. Stage 3 involves coding the interviews. This time-consuming exercise requires identifying the key themes in the interviews and marking them on the hard text and/or creating relevant files on your computer. You could have primary themes and sub-themes. The themes selected will be dependent on the interview material, your interview guide, the research questions and existing research, concepts and theory. Once you have coded your interviews you need to select the themes you are going to focus on (stage 4). This is often determined by the richness of the data in a particular theme, existing research and the concepts/theoretical framework that you will be using. Stage 5 is the actual writing up of the interview material using the material in the themes selected. Various suggestions are given as to how to create a lively and solid write-up. Vignettes/profiles as a powerful way of presenting interview material is discussed. The chapter concludes with a discussion of the strengths and potential pitfalls of computer-assisted qualitative data analysis software (CAQDAS).

Exercise

Transcribing and analysing your interviews

Transcribe an interview you have conducted. Once you have transcribed it go through it utilising the five stages reviewed for analysing and writing up your interviews. Note down the themes and sub-themes identified and begin the process of writing up your interviews using the relevant themes and sub-themes.

REFERENCES

Appleton, J.V. (1995) 'Analysing qualitative interview data: addressing issues of validity and reliability', *Journal of Advanced Nursing*, 22 (5): 993–7.

Clark, A., Georgellis, Y. and Sanford, A. (2001) 'Scarring: the psychological impact of unemployment', *Economica*, 68 (270): 221–41.

Connell, R.W. (1995) *Masculinities*. London: Polity Press.

Ezzy, D. (2002) *Qualitative Analysis: Practice and Innovation*. London: Routledge.

Humble, A.M. (2012) Qualitative data analysis software: a call for understanding, detail, intentionality, and thoughtfulness', *Journal of Family Theory & Review*, 4 (June): 122–37.

King, N. and Horrocks, C. (2012) *Interviews in Qualitative Research*. London: SAGE.

Kvale, S. and Brinkmann, S. (2009) *Interviews: Learning the Craft of Qualitative Research Interviewing*. London: SAGE.

McDowell, L. (2003) *Redundant Masculinities? Employment Change and White Working Class Youth*. Oxford: Blackwell.

Miles, M.B. (1979) 'Qualitative data as an attractive nuisance: the problem of analysis', *Administrative Science Quarterly*, 24 (4): 590–601.

Miles, M.B. and Huberman, A.M. (1994) *Qualitative Data Analysis: An Expanded Sourcebook*. Thousand Oaks, CA: SAGE.

Morris, A. and Wilson, S. (2014) 'Struggling on the Newstart unemployment benefit in Australia: the experience of a neoliberal form of employment assistance', *Economic Labour Relations Review*, 25 (2): 202–21.

Rapley, T.J. (2001) 'The art(fullness) of open-ended interviewing: some considerations on analysing interviews', *Qualitative Research*, 1 (3): 303–23.

Roulston, K., De Marrais, K. and Lewis, J.B. (2003) 'Learning to interview in the social sciences', *Qualitative Inquiry*, 9 (4): 643–68.

Rubin, H.J. and Rubin, I.S. (2012) *Qualitative Interviewing: The Art of Hearing Data*. Los Angeles: SAGE.

Saldana, J. (2012) *Coding Manual for Qualitative Researchers*. London: SAGE.

Seale, C. and Rivas, C. (2012) 'Using software to analyse qualitative interviews', in J.F. Gubrium, J.A. Holstein, A.B. Marvasti and K.D. McKinney (eds), *The SAGE Handbook of Interview Research: The Complexity of the Craft*. Los Angeles: SAGE. pp. 427–40.

Seidman, I. (2013) *Interviewing as Qualitative Research*. New York: Teachers College Press.

Weis, L. (1990) *Working Class Without Work: High School Students in a Deindustrialising Economy*. London: Routledge.

Wilson, W.J. (1996) *When Work Disappears: The World of the New Urban Poor*. New York: Alfred A. Knopf.

INDEX

Note: Figures and Tables are indicated by page numbers in bold.

Abraham, Margaret 54, 56, 64
abused African American women 54, 56, 64
abused South Asian women in USA 54, 56, 64
access to interviewees 60–2
  in 'total institutions' 62, 62n1
accuracy of responses 7
Adamson, S. and Holloway, M. 102–3
African-American women re-entering
    education 108
Aldridge, J. and Medina, J. 22
analysis 124–33
  interview-data-as-topic 124–5
  interview-data-resource 124
  computer-assisted qualitative data analysis
      software (CAQDAS) 135–6
  quality of interview data 132
  questions about interviews 131
  reflective 125
  stages
    1 read-through and note-taking 126–7
    2 notable quotes 127
    3 coding/themes 127–30
    4 selecting themes 130
    5 interpreting and writing up data 130–3
  starting point 125–6
  thematic approach 125
anonymity 21–3, 95
appointments 72–3
  and punctuality 76
ATLAs 135
audio recording 69–70, 70–1, 81, 122
  reluctant interviewees 100
Australia: Corrective Services Act 2000 62

background noise 74
Barone, J.T. and Switzer, J.Y. 50
Belousov, K. et al 101
bereavement 102
Bergman, M.M. 9
bias 9–10, 106
  see also interviews across difference
black activists in Soweto 108
body language 82–3
Bogardus, Emory 2
Booth, Charles 1–2
Brett, R. and Specht, I. 6
Briggs, C.L. 115

cancer patients: 'end of life issues and identity' 61
CAQDAS packages 135–6
Cashmore, J.A. and Parkinson, P.N. 5–6
Chicana women interviewed by Chicana and
    Anglo women 107
child soldiers 6
children 24
Clark, Taliaferro 18
coding 127–8, 135–6
coercion 23
Columbia University: ethics guidelines 20
community-based participatory research
    (CBPR) 109–10
complementary methods 9
concluding the interview 90
confidentiality and anonymity 21–2, 81–2, 103
  with audio recording 70–1
consent *see* informed consent
constructivist approaches 12–13

Contact Orders Programs 5–6
'contextual factors' 73
Cook, C. 95

dangers: ambient and situational 100–2
   females researchers studying seafarer
     communities 101
   'frontier zones' 101
   research on health and safety in shipping 101
   strategies 102
data saturation 64
Davies, P. 73, 74
'defended subjects' 11
disabled people 24, 111–12
discourse analysis 69
distance interviews 92–6
distress to interviewees 23, 26, 32, 102
domestic violence 103, 107, 111
dress of interviewers 76–7
Dropbox 70
Dyck, I. 107

Economic and Social Research Council (ESRC) 19
elites 57, 113
Ellis, Carolyn 22
email interviews 4, 94–6
   advantages/disadvantages 95
   setting up 96
encryption software 22–3
equipment 69–71, 122
Esterberg, K.G. 74
ethics 17–34
   care 33–4
   children 24
   'ethical mindfulness' 32
   ethics application 19, 25–9
     consent form **28–9**, 72
     Ethics Committee requests and response
       29–31
     information sheet 26–**8**
   Indigenous communities 25
   issues arising in interviews 31–2
   and journalists 19
   key principles 19–25
     avoidance of harm 23–5
     confidentiality and anonymity 21–2, 32–3
     independence of research 25
     informed consent 18, 20–1, 28–9

ethics *cont.*
   integritiy of research 20
   voluntary participation 23
   need for consideration of ethics 17–19
   payment of interviewees 60
   in qualitative research 18–19
   sexual abuse of Aboriginal children 21
   vulnerable groups 23–4
   writing up the interview 32–3
ethnicity 107, 108
explaining research to interviewees 72, 81

failed/failing interviews 103–6
   strategies to rescue 104–6, 105
Fallaci, Oriana 113
females researchers studying seafarer
   communities 101
feminist research 106
filmmaking project for LGBTIQ community 91
Flick, U. 40
follow up interviews 90–1
Fontana, A. and Frey, J.H. 82, 91
free association 11
Freud, Sigmund 2
Frey, J.H. and Oishi, S.M. 49

gatekeepers 60–2
gender 9, 10, 106–7
   and ethnicity 107
generalisability 7
girls with anorexia nervosa 23
Glaser, B.G. and Strauss, A. 64
Goffman, Erving 62n1, 80, 82
Google Hangouts 94
GoToMeeting 94
grounded theory 41
Guest, G. et al 64
Guillemin, M. and Gillam, L. 32

Halse, C. and Honey, A. 23, 26
Hanckel, Benjamin 91, 110–11
Hanna, P. 92
harm to interviewees and researchers 23–5
Head, E. 60
health and safety in shipping 101
Helsinki Declaration 18
history of interviewing 1–3
Holloway, W. and Jefferson, T. 11

home interviews 74, 75–6
homeless people: role of dignity 56
Housing and Accommodation Support
    Initiative (HASI) 75
housing tenure of pensioners 46–9, 127, 128–9,
    134–6
Howell, N. 101

impact of unemployment **45–6**
independence of research 25
Indigenous communities 109–10
information sheets 72
informed consent 18, 20–1, 81–2
    and children 24
    consent forms **28–9**, 72
        refusal to sign 100
        storage 124
    signing the form 21
inner-city transition in Johannesburg 9, 41, 64
internet
    cloud storage 70
    email interviews 94–6
    online software interviews 4, 71, 92, 94
    recruitment of interviewees 59
interruptions 84–5
interview guides 39–51
    detail 39–40
    examples
        housing tenure of pensioners 46–9
        impact of unemployment **45–6**
    framing questions 50
    logical progression 49
    order of questions 49
    research question 40–1
    topics and questions 43–6
interviewer-interviewee relationship 12, 13, 49
    body language 82–3, 89
    developing rapport 71–2, 79–83
    first meeting 81–2
    gender 106–7
    power relationships 106
    see also interviews across difference
interviewers' self-disclosure 91–2, 106
interviews across difference
    disabled people 111–12
    elites 113
    ethnicity 107, 108
    gender 106–7

interviews across difference *cont.*
    Indigenous communities 109–10
    marginalised and disadvantaged 114–15
    race 108–9
    second language speakers 112–13
    sexual orientation 110–11

Johnson-Bailey, J. 108

Kendall, M. et al 61
key principles 21–2
King, N. and Horrocks, C. 61, 131–2
Kitchin, R. 111
knowledge of interviewee 81, 113
knowledge of research area 40, 113, 114
knowledge workers 11
Kvale, S. and Brinkmann, S. 3, 126, 132, 133

LaSala, M.C. 110
Lee, R.M. 100
Leech, B.L. 50
length of interview 4
LGBT community 110
life histories 11–12
limitations of interviews **7**
longitudinal studies 4

McClennen, J.C. 111
MacDougall, C. and Fudge, E. 57
Maori and Pacific Islanders: failed interview 114
marginalised and disadvantaged 114–15
Marks, M. 108
Marshall, M.N. 63
Marzano, M. 33
MaxQDA 135
Meadows, L.M. et al 110
meeting an interviewee 71–2
Meho, L.I. 95
Mengele, Josef 18
Miles, M.B. 126
Miller, A.N. and Keys, C. 56
Miller, J. and Brunson, R.K. 10
Miller, K.R. 112–13
Minichiello, V. et al 79
misleading responses 2, 7
misunderstanding questions 105
multiple interviews 4
Murray, C.D. and Sixsmith, J. 95

Nairn, K. et al 114
narrative interviews 11
Nash, Shonrah 54, 56, 64
National Statement on Ethical Conduct in
    Human Research 24
Nazi experiments 18
neutrality of interviewer 91
note-taking 70
number of interviewees 64
Nuremberg Code 18
NVivo 135

Oakley, A. 91, 106
    Becoming a Mother 106
occasions for interviewing 8–9
Oliver, M. and Barnes, C. 111
order of questions 83–4

Pahl, Ray: *After Success* 63
Patton, M.Q. 44
payment to interviewees 23, 60
pharmaceutical companies 25
Pittaway, E. et al 24
politicians 113
Prior, M. 112
prison release practices in Australia 62
probing 3, **87**–9, 104–5
profiles of interviewees 122, **123**
prosthetic users email interviews 95
psychoanalysis 2
punctuality 76

qualitative data analysis software (QDAS) 135–6
questionnaires 8, 9
questions 43–4, 85–7, **86**
    leading questions 86
    opinions/values 44
    order 83–4
    phrasing 50, 86, 105
    probing **87**–9
    rephrasing 105
    types
        background questions 45
        experience/behaviour 44
        feelings 44
        knowledge 44
        sensory questions 45

race 9–10, 55, 108–9
race and Hurricane Katrina 109
Rapley, T.J. 124–5
Raudonis, B.M. 24
realist perspectives 12
recruitment of interviewees 55–8
    by gatekeepers 61
    elites 57
    key contacts 57
    snowball method 58
    steps to finding **57–8**
    survey questionnaires 58–9
    through advertising 59–60
    using Internet 59
    winning trust 56
refugees 24
representative samples of interviewees 62–3
research questions 40–1
    homeless youth in Melbourne 40–1
reticent interviewees 85, 103–4
Rhodes, P.J. 108
Richards, D. 57, 77
risk assessments 101–2
Roulston, K. 105, 122
Rubin, H.J. and Rubin, I.S. 6, 107, 127, 132

St Louis armed robbers 58
St Louis gang members 10
Sampson, H. and Thomas, H. 101
School Board Visitors (SBVs) 1–2
Schultze, U. 11
second language speakers 112–13
security 75–6, 93
    and danger 100–2
Seidman, I. 126
Seldon, A. 113
selection of interviewees 53–4
selection of material 20, 33
semi-structured interviews 3, 10
sensitive topics 8, 74, 80, 86, 102–3
    impact on interviewer 103
setting up interviews 71–3
sexual orientation 110–11
Shakespeare, Tom 112
Skype 4, 71, 92, 94
Smith, L.T. 107
snowball method of recruitment 58

South Africa 9, 41, 64, 108
standardisation 9
storage
    consent forms 124
    of data 22–3
    interviews 124
strengths of interviews 5–6, **7**
Stroebe, M. et al 102
structured interviews 9–10
Sturges, J.E. and Hanrahan, K.J. 94
surveys 6, 8
    Australian attitudes to inequality 8
    Australian unemployment benefits 6
    response rate 58–9
    to recruit interviewees 58–9

telephone interviews 4, 71, 72, 92–4
    quality 94
themes 128–30
Thomas, W.I.: *The Polish Peasant in Europe and America* 2
Tixier y Vigil, Y. and Elasser, N. 107
transcribing 121–4
    'correcting' language 122
    noting quality of interview 122
    profiles of interviewees 122, **123**
trust 80, 104
Tuskegee syphilis study 17–18
types of interviews 9–12

unemployment benefits in Australia (Newstart) 6, 131
university settings 74–5, 114
unstructured interviews 10–11

venues 72, 73–6
    comfort 74–5
    for marginalised people 114
    quietness 73–4
    security for interviewer 75–6
verification of responses 7
Viber 94
vignettes 133–5
voluntary participation 23
vulnerable groups 23–4

Walsh, T. 62
Wasserfall, R. 106–7
Wengraf, T. 44
Wilson, S. and Meagher, G. 8
women at risk from HIV in Nigeria and Kenya 64
women with sexually transmitted viruses 95
Wright, R.T. and Decker, S.H. 58
writing up 130–3
    accuracy 33
    common threads 131
    confidentiality 32–3
    guide 133
    overarching themes 131–2
    quotes selection 132
    reflecting material 132
    vignettes 133–5

young Nigerian men in armed groups 6
Young, Pauline V.: *Scientific Social Surveys and Research* 3

Zuckerman, H. 57